Praise for *Chasing Moments*

Chasing Moments is a must read for every Christian and for anyone seeking a more meaningful existence. In an engaging style, Malone sets forth the essentials needed for a mature Christian life. His basic theme is that the only true existence is one fully surrendered to, and guided by, the Creator who designed it in the first place. Malone is especially concerned about those who claim to be Christian but live an existence more conformed to the ways of the world than to God; he warns that such an orientation is to follow the broad path leading to destruction and to miss the narrow path leading to life.

Treating numerous biblical texts to illustrate his themes, Malone's interpretation of Scripture is consistently sound and clearly presented. He has a knack for taking biblical metaphors and parables and retelling them with modern examples. Even when the subject matters are the profound issues of life and death, he consistently draws from his own personal experiences—farming, his eight-year-old grandson, golf, his dogs, and the like. This makes for engaging reading.

Appropriately, the author's final chapter deals with the concept of *zoe,* the Greek word used in the Gospel of John to speak of spiritual life—life in God, as opposed to mere existence. In John's Gospel, zoe is the only true life there is, and this hold true for the earthly life as well as that to come. One who does not have this zoe-life is *already* dead. Malone weaves this theme throughout his book: without the zoe life that comes from God and lives in God, one has no real life—but simply exists. The world is full of these mere "existers"—in the pews, as well as on the streets. They need to read this book.

JOHN POLHILL, SENIOR PROFESSOR OF NEW TESTAMENT INTERPRETATION,
THE SOUTHERN BAPTIST THEOLOGICAL SEMINARY; AUTHOR
ACTS, NEW AMERICAN COMMENTARY (NASHVILLE: BROADMAN PRESS, 1992) AND
PAUL AND HIS LETTERS (NASHVILLE: BROADMAN/HOLMAN PUBLISHERS, 1999)

Through careful biblical exposition and narrative clarity, *Chasing Moments* invites us to rest in God's presence, wonder at His majesty and live our lives with eternal purpose. With the wisdom of a pastor-farmer, Ed Malone takes us to his farm in Tennessee, where we walk freshly tilled earth, lift bales of sweet, dry, hay, return a lost calf to its mother, and welcome a young boy into manhood—all with an eye toward better understanding God's eternal purpose for our lives. A book for all ages, *Chasing Moments* will remind you of who you are in Christ, so you can live, with purpose, the days to come.

RICHARD A. MAXSON, PHD, ASSOCIATE PROFESSOR OF COMMUNICATION, DRURY UNIVERSITY, MO; DR. MAXSON SPENDS HIS SUMMERS TEACHING AT AN INDIANA YOUTH CAMP AND AT LITHUANIA CHRISTIAN COLLEGE IN LITHUANIA.

Chasing Moments invites you to enter into the Kingdom of God; to choose the narrow gate and walk with the Savior; to pursue a deeper, fuller, more meaningful Christian life. In presenting this invitation, Ed Malone follows the example of Jesus, the master teacher. From wrestling a calf in an ice-cold creek to fighting the weeds that would consume a hay field, Ed uses everyday stories from the farm and other parts of his life to illustrate principles of kingdom living. He masterfully presents the seemingly paradoxical concepts that "you can only have life by dying to yourself" and "true freedom is gained only by becoming a servant and slave to the King."

Having taught in the classroom for years, I find Ed's teaching style engaging and effective. *Chasing Moments* would be beneficial for both new and mature Christians desiring to deepen and enrich their life in the Kingdom. The end of chapter questions and challenges make this a great book for group study in a Sunday school class or Bible study.

TIM DEAN, PHD, ASSOCIATE PROFESSOR, TENNESSEE TECH UNIVERSITY

Perhaps you are craving something deeper than the life you have experienced so far, something more than just chasing moments, something with quality and eternal significance. In this book, you will find that adventures beyond description and life in all its fullness are waiting for you, if you are willing to relinquish control of your life to someone who can manage your life better than you can—to God, who wants to have a personal relationship with you. Ed's analogies of farming, mountain trails, and others, make this book real, practical, and easy to apply to life's journey. The questions for reflection at the end of each chapter make it a useful book to study as a small group.

JEAN FLOYD, MA, INTERCULTURAL STUDIES AND TEACHING ENGLISH AS A FOREIGN LANGUAGE, COLUMBIA INTERNATIONAL UNIVERSITY; CHURCH PLANTER IN PARAGUAY FOR FIFTEEN YEARS; ALONG WITH HER HUSBAND, TONY, AND THEIR THREE CHILDREN, NOW SERVING AS MISSIONARY WITH SIM

ED MALONE

CHASING MOMENTS

WILL I LIVE LIFE…OR SIMPLY EXIST?

Deep River
B O O K S

Published by Deep River Books
PO box 310
Sisters, Oregon 97759
541-549-1139
www.deepriverbooks.com

ISBN-13: 9781937756727
ISBN-10: 1937756726

Library of Congress. 2012954326

Cover design by David Litwin, Purefusion Media

Contents

Acknowledgments

Bill Carmichael and his team at Deep River Books worked diligently to polish and shape *Chasing Moments* into the best form possible. I am humbled by their partnership and thankful for their input and expertise.

I am indebted to Terry Sims for helping me see the value of using my farm analogies to carry spiritual principles. Terry was in the later stages of cancer when she agreed to look at my first splash of ideas for a book. Terry's insight into good writing helped me focus the central thrust for the book.

Angela, Joy, and Laurie were brave enough to help me hammer through the foundation and basic structure of the original manuscript. Over several months, Cathy Streiner provided editorial help in bringing the book into the form sufficient to secure the interest of Deep River Books. Cathy kept me in touch with how the reader might receive what I wrote and worked diligently in helping me craft my writing style.

Over several decades, my ability to understand the kingdom message has been developed by being a pastor. Through the investment of many, I have been given the opportunity to study and hone my skills as a communicator of the gospel. To all of you, I say thank you.

To my wife, Gale, who endured all of my late-night writing and rewriting. I acknowledge that her encouragement and patience were what enabled me to "finish the race."

Introduction

We live in an amazing world. Rich variety is expressed in our food, clothing styles, architecture, languages, occupations, and religious expressions. Yet, despite our diverse cultures and the unique ways we human beings spend our days, we all strive for all that life might offer. Blaise Pascal, a devout Christian and accomplished mathematician of the seventeenth century, wrote, "All men seek happiness. This is without exception. Whatever different means they employ, they all tend to this end."

In this search for life—full, real life—many grasp for individual moments of fulfillment and consequently live in a never-ending quest. A cruise or exotic dinner promises pleasure but ends quickly without any sustained satisfaction. Surely life is more than chasing moments! Life leaves many of us empty in the end. No one should neglect the question to find out whether life has ultimate meaning. The question is this: "Will I live life or simply exist?"

The classic phrase "the blind leading the blind" identifies a key obstacle preventing the enjoyment of life's true meaning. Long before most people ever ask the right questions about life, they're already following the same path as nearly everyone else. Leaders tend to groom those who come behind them to follow in what they have learned from those who went before. No one knows if, why, or how the path they're on will lead to a truly fulfilled life. Few are brave enough to consider that so many could be so wrong.

The essence of what Jesus came to do is expressed in his statement, "I have come that they may have life, and have it to the full" (John 10:10b). Jesus invites each of us to "Enter through the narrow gate. For wide is the gate and broad is the road that leads to destruction, and many enter through it. But small is the gate and narrow the road that leads to life, and only a few find it" (Matthew 7: 13–14).

According to Jesus, the path to life is not the one most people travel.

No one accidentally winds up on it. A personal and intentional decision to leave the broad highway must be made in order to find life.

It is alarming to hear Jesus say that only a few find the small gate to life. It is even more startling to hear him say, "Not everyone who says to me, 'Lord, Lord,' will enter the kingdom of heaven, but only he who does the will of my Father who is in heaven" (Matthew 7:21).

What separates the masses from the few Jesus speaks of who find the small gate to life? Based on the teaching of Jesus, are you certain you've done more than just say, "Lord, Lord"?

This book centers on the life-changing and life-fulfilling message of Jesus. His teachings offer help for putting into practice a vibrant faith that is not just a way to believe, but rather a life-giving way to live.

For those of you who have been around the things of God but find that your faith has failed to enliven you as it should, this book seeks to introduce you to the magnificence of life in God's kingdom. To those already committed to the narrow road, I humbly offer you the opportunity to look at the kingdom from the viewpoint of another traveler. God intends for us to enrich one another's lives as we share our common experience. If you are a seeker with unanswered questions about life's purpose and especially what it means to follow Jesus, please allow this book to help you search further.

Much is at stake. Only a few see what others miss. This is your opportunity to both see and enter into the fullness of life in God's kingdom.

Chapter One

What Is Worth Everything?

EVERY HUMAN BEING HAS BEEN GIVEN an opportunity called life. Many race along seeking pleasure and fulfillment, while the road makes others stagger. Most travelers simply follow the accepted patterns of living without questioning. To the side of this road, Jesus puts up a sign:

WARNING

The road you are traveling leads off a cliff.
There is a small gate with a narrow road that
leads to life, and only a few find it.

PROCEED WITH CAUTION

"Is that it, Jesus?" we ask. "Aren't you leaving out a few important details?" In the 1800s, when miners came out of California announcing gold, everyone wanted to know where to find it and how hard or dangerous it was to access. It would seem that Jesus's sign should provide further instructions: "You will find this small gate three miles ahead on the right side of the road next to a white oak tree across from an old red barn."

Yet Jesus's sign is more revealing than we realize at first glance. Let's look more closely. Clearly, the world's way of life won't give us what we're seeking. No one will be swept down the road to life by joining a large, moving crowd. The road starts at a small gate, implying that a personal choice is required. Since only a few find the gate, we must look with a different set of eyes to notice this unique entry point leading to life. Jesus

describes the road as narrow, which alerts us to travel challenges. Caution is appropriate, because failure to enter this gate carries enormous consequences.

A TREETOP VIEW

I remember the first time I noticed the small gate and the narrow road beyond it. As a young boy, I enjoyed climbing to the top of a big silver-leaf maple in our front yard. There I had a private sanctuary and a view that brought my world into sharp perspective.

From my vantage point, I saw a manufacturing plant that employed thousands of people. I could also see our local church, the high school, the duck pond—which was a great fishing hole—and the cattle on the farm around my home. As I lay high in the branches, I was fascinated watching the clouds pass by against the backdrop of an infinite sky.

Everything that came into view prompted me to ask questions: *What does all this mean? How do I fit into the hustle and bustle going on beneath my tree? Does it all make sense? Do people know where they are going and why?* When I looked at the sky in all its wonder, I considered the possibility that something might lie beyond what I could see. It was an inkling, an idea—the small gate.

People passed by beneath my tree, going about their lives. Life seemed disturbingly orchestrated by directives about how to live and what mattered in life. At my age, these markers were loud and clear: sports, girls, money, and popularity were offered as the golden rings of happiness. With the passing of time, the focus shifted to the theme of making all the money you can to accumulate all the stuff you can so as to be amply prepared for a life of ease in retirement. Surely there's more to life than laboring long and hard with the desperate hope of a few good years at the end!

For others, the Epicurean mantra of "eat, drink, and be merry for tomorrow you may die" was the full assessment of life's meaning. Such thinking reduces life to a purely selfish act of consumption without meaning or purpose. In the face of a variety of opinions, the challenge was to not get lost in the thinking going on beneath my tree.

In our unique, individual ways, most of us have had similar experiences of questioning the meaning of life. The words of Isaiah the prophet describe these moments: "Whether you turn to the right or to the left, your ears will hear a voice behind you, saying, 'This is the way; walk in it'" (Isaiah 30:21).

One thing was for sure. Having felt the pull of God, I would never be the same.

BIGGER THAN LIFE

That boy in the tree had a lot of questions, but not enough answers. He was young, questioning, inexperienced, and naïve like so many of us have been or still are. Many sense the narrow road beckoning, and yet, they do not find the pull compelling enough to respond. Thankfully, the pull is not a one-time experience. Over time and after continued investigation, the true value of the road can become clear, bringing with it hope and a strong incentive to respond more fully.

The pull of the road of life is the drawing of God, a prodding which questions our view of life's meaning and purpose. When we're sensitive to it, the awareness of something bigger than life presses upon us and at the same time beckons to us through the wonder of the world in which we live. Some ignore or reject God's drawing. Others respond to the pull.

Simon Peter followed Jesus closely for several years, observing what he did and taught. Those around Jesus viewed him as everything from a prophet to a demoniac. But Peter did not let the noise of the crowd drown out the pull of God. As he spent time with Jesus, God's presence took Peter's awareness beyond the crowd's assessment.

Jesus asked his disciples directly how they perceived him: "'But what about you?' he asked. 'Who do you say I am?' Simon Peter answered, 'You are the Christ, the Son of the living God'" (Matthew 16:15–16). Jesus affirmed Peter's response and told him that his answer had not been revealed to him by man, but by God the Father. Like Peter, our assessment and response to Jesus depend on our sensitivity to God.

Another example of sensitivity to God's pull is revealed in the story

of Moses and the burning bush. After killing an Egyptian, Moses fled from Egypt and was living in the wilderness. God used a burning bush to get his attention.

What started as the very natural event of a bush on fire became an occasion of communication between God and Moses. "Moses saw that though the bush was on fire it did not burn up. So Moses thought, 'I will go over and see this strange sight—why the bush does not burn up'" (Exodus 3:2b–3). Moses could have ignored and walked away from God's special pull on his life. However, questioning can lead to answers if we diligently seek to respond to that which beckons to us.

Some consider that the reality of God is validated only if he acts in ways that are overwhelming. Elijah the prophet hid in a cave in fear of Jezebel's threat to kill him. As he hid in the cave, there was a strong wind, an earthquake, and a fire, but the Lord was not in these. Instead, he spoke to Elijah in a still, small voice (1 Kings 19:12). If we expect God to use a spectacular event to get our attention, we might very well miss his approach to our lives.

Jeremiah reminds us that sincerity of effort is required when seeking God: "You will seek me and find me when you seek me with all your heart" (Jeremiah 29:13).

Thankfully, Moses did not ignore God's attempt to get his attention. Elijah's experience of the still small voice of God will be true for most of us as well. God requires our response, our seeking. An occasional inquiry or halfhearted effort will not achieve results in this endeavor. Hebrews 11:6 says, "And without faith it is impossible to please God, because anyone who comes to him must believe that he exists and that he rewards those who earnestly seek him."

In those early attempts to understand life from the treetop, I was drawn to investigate something of greater value than I could ever imagine. Jesus's call to respond to the pull of the small gate and travel the narrow road is an invitation to become part of God's kingdom—a realm where we enjoy a relationship with God that fulfills the meaning and purpose of life.

THE PEARL OF GREAT VALUE

Jesus describes the value of life in God's kingdom this way: "Again, the kingdom of heaven is like a merchant looking for fine pearls. When he found one of great value, he went away and sold everything he had and bought it" (Matthew 13:45–46).

Jesus uses the value of pearls to mirror the importance of being in God's kingdom. Today, pearls lack the level of value they had in biblical times. Therefore, Jesus's words might not be very forceful to us—but they spoke loudly to his original audience.

For centuries, pearls commanded prices that were unfathomable. A story is told that the Roman general Vitellius financed an entire military campaign by selling just one of his mother's pearl earrings. Today, pearls are regarded as inexpensive accessories. What happened to devalue something that was once held in such high regard?

The perceived value of pearls diminished drastically when a process was developed for making what are called *cultured pearls*. A cultured pearl has a few layers of actual pearl material on the outside, but the core and much of the volume of the pearl consist of a man-made substitute. The once near-miraculous event of finding a natural pearl in an oyster on the ocean floor became less significant, and the price of pearls plummeted. Today, a string of pearls no longer makes an impression, since most people do not know or even care whether a necklace is made of natural, cultured, or even imitation pearls. Only the owner knows whether the price was paid for the real thing.

AUTHENTIC PEARL, ETERNAL VALUE

The pull I felt called me to something eternal, larger than life, and worth more than the finest pearl ever found. It was real, offered to me from God. Yet I hesitated, unsure of what to do.

In retrospect, I am alarmed at how easy it would have been to dismiss my treetop experiences. I could have quit asking questions about the meaning of life, taking life at face value and joining everyone else in the pursuit of all my natural world had to offer. After all, the promise of fame, pleasure, and fortune are hard to resist.

I faced the age-old dilemma of not putting the cart in front of the horse. The challenge was to let the meaning and purpose of life pull me rather than focusing on making a living and only occasionally having time to think about life's meaning. Taking care of the necessities of life can be so consuming that life is absorbed by this effort and even defined by how well the goal is achieved. Jesus's words are direct in addressing this issue: "Therefore I tell you do not worry about your life, what you will eat or drink; or about your body, what you will wear. Is not life more important than food, and the body more important than clothes?" (Matthew 6:25).

Certainly we must tend to life's needs. The issue is what comes first. The pursuit of God is primary and able to shape everything that follows. We would do well to remember the words of Jesus: "What good will it be for a man if he gains the whole world, yet forfeits his soul? Or what can a man give in exchange for his soul?" (Matthew 16:26).

All of life needs to be a continual pursuit of answers to our questions as we respond to God rather than ignore him. For me, it took a lot of searching and listening before the priceless pearl came fully into view.

WORTH LIFE ITSELF

The parable of the pearl is not a piece of idealistic philosophy or exaggerated hyperbole. Jesus used this parable to emphasize the magnitude of what it means to be in God's kingdom. Since biblical times and into the present, an innumerable host of people have actively demonstrated that the kingdom of God is truly priceless.

Many have given their lives rather than deny the pull of God, which for them was larger and more important than life itself. What did they experience that was so valuable, so worthy of commitment, that they were willing to pay such a high price? If you or I were faced with the same demand, would we have the courage to follow their example? Most people make a little room for religion but are far from the level of commitment that values a relationship with God more than life.

There are numerous examples both in the Scriptures and in church history of those who willingly gave their lives for the cause of the king-

dom. Even with Jesus's warning that he would die as a martyr, Peter spent his years helping the early church emerge as a force never to be extinguished. Dietrich Bonheoffer was not in his homeland of Germany when World War II broke out, but he voluntarily returned and died trying to speak out against the evil forces in control of his homeland. Even today, in places all over the world, more people are dying for the faith in this generation than at any other time in church history. The many who give their lives for the kingdom are a challenge to those who only embrace Christianity when it is religiously convenient.

Cultured and imitation pearls have been quite successful in the marketplace. Many are unwilling to pay the price for the real thing, and others could care less whether their pearls are authentic as long as they make an impression. When it comes to one's spiritual response to life, settling for something that looks like the real thing has eternal consequences. Just as man's manipulation of pearl production radically altered the pearl market, humanity's distortion of Christianity has produced religious forms that are far removed from the kingdom message Jesus gave. Unfortunately, within Christianity there are many religious expressions that have a pearl surface but a man-made core.

SPIRITUAL AUTHENTICITY

Cultured pearls were not around during the time of Jesus. However, he often addressed the lack of authenticity in religious expressions. Jesus quoted the Old Testament prophet Isaiah when speaking to the scribes and Pharisees:

> He replied, "Isaiah was right when he prophesied about you hypocrites; as it is written: 'These people honor me with their lips, but their hearts are far from me. They worship me in vain; their teachings are but rules taught by men.'" (Mark 7:6–7)

Jesus described these religious people with the word "hypocrite," which means actor. Actors present themselves as people they are not. Similarly, offering lip service (saying the right words) is far removed from

having a heart connection with God. The scribes and Pharisees had a cultured-pearl form of religion that looked real on the outside. In actuality, their focus was outward compliance and rules taught by men rather than heartfelt worship based on knowing and loving God.

In another setting, Jesus addressed the teachers of the law and the Pharisees with these words: "Woe to you, teachers of the law and Pharisees, you hypocrites! You are like whitewashed tombs, which look beautiful on the outside but on the inside are full of dead men's bones and everything unclean. In the same way, on the outside you appear to people as righteous but on the inside you are full of hypocrisy and wickedness" (Matthew 23:27–28).

Jesus identified the actors for what they were: cultured pearls with a beautifully fabricated pearl exterior and a man-made core. It was obvious to Jesus that, in their hearts, these religious people were not truly connected to God. They were confident their relationship with God should be held up as an example to the world, but they were committed to religious forms instead of to God himself. The religious traditions given to them by previous generations substituted for true relationship with God. Not only did these leaders fail to enter the small gate, but they and other religious actors of every generation also caused—and still cause—many to reject God on the basis of hypocritical, man-made religion.

Like the leadership of the Jews in Jesus's day, it is possible to think you believe in God, hold absolute reverence for the Scriptures, pray, fast, give alms, and attend special worship meetings with an accompanying concert of music, and yet in the end find yourself calling for the death of Jesus. For them, things looked good on the outside; however, the true goal was a changed heart evidenced by a changed life—and they missed it.

Religion vs Relationship

The pearl of infinite value is not obtained through the cheap "I believe in God" investment many think is enough to give. A number of modern religious expressions claiming to be part of Christianity encourage people to focus on getting what they want ("What's in it for me?") rather than

the chance of a lifetime to respond to God's offer of love, relationship, and life in his kingdom.

The small gate and narrow road do not lead to religion, but rather to a relationship with God; and there is only one such gate, one such road. Jesus's rejection of those who were religious on the outside proves that false religion is but one of the many lanes the crowd is traveling on the broad highway that leads to destruction.

BECOMING A PEARL MERCHANT

Search with the diligence of a pearl merchant, and don't be fooled by substitutes. The Scriptures are God's unique gift to us, serving as our road map for this journey. It doesn't matter how many books you read, sermons you hear, or songs you listen to, until the Bible is in your lap as a time of personal interaction with God, only small steps can be made. By personal study of the Scriptures, a supernatural event of participation with God is available to all who seek to know him better.

Moses described to Israel the pull of God in this way:

> Now what I am commanding you today is not too difficult for you or beyond your reach. It is not up in heaven, so that you have to ask, "Who will ascend into heaven to get it and proclaim it to us so we may obey it?" Nor is it beyond the sea, so that you have to ask, "Who will cross the sea to get it and proclaim it to us so we may obey it?" No, the word is very near you; it is in your mouth and in your heart so you may obey it. (Deuteronomy 30:11–14)

If we are willing to listen, God will lead us in the way that we should go in pursuit of his kingdom.

ONE OF A KIND

The priceless pearl of the kingdom is unique, truly one of a kind. This pearl you will never own. It will own you, but only if you are willing to pay the price. Selling what owns you in terms of attachment to this world

opens you to the opportunity to be owned by God.

Because only a few find the small gate and narrow road to life, it is important to climb high enough in your tree to get away from the noise of the broad highway and feel the special pull of God. It requires courage to venture through the gate into the spiritual world many deny or even ridicule. The crowds will call to you, asking you to stay with them on the broad road so they can be comfortable. They'll claim that only the silly or uninformed dare venture onto anything but the mainstream path. You have the option of turning a deaf ear to them.

Peter listened to God rather than those around him when he assessed who Jesus was. It is now your turn. The power of God's presence confronts each of us and calls for a decision. It is not a hard choice for those who recognize the worth of what so many fail to pursue.

REFLECTING ON CHAPTER 1

What does the world proclaim will give you life? How is this message announced? How do these life-giving promises of the world fall short of the true life offered by Jesus?

You might have experienced a time when you felt the pull of God and the opportunity to ignore or seek him. What have your personal "treetop experiences" been like?

What, if anything, has helped you to see the kingdom of God more fully as a priceless pearl?

Chapter Two

Giving Up the Right to Rule

THE FAMILIAR SAYING "If it wasn't for bad luck, I wouldn't have any luck at all" seems to be foundational to the news media. Most of the time, if it wasn't for bad news, there wouldn't be any news at all. At times I prefer not to read the paper or listen to the news to avoid being inundated with all the mess going on in our world. An occasional break in a news report might highlight someone's courage or exceptional expression of kindness, but these are deviations from the usual gloom.

The phrase "bad luck" is an oxymoron, a figure of speech that combines contradictory terms. Sayings like "this sure is a fine mess" or "let's agree to disagree" are similar. At first glance, Jesus seems to create an oxymoron when he invites us to enter God's kingdom and calls his offer "good news."

Entering a kingdom where there is already a king can be risky—particularly in modern times, when freedom and autonomy are valued so highly. Having a choice about entering makes the offer even more difficult. How will I fit into this kingdom? Will there be hard times or good? What are the benefits and demands? Will things be better than the way they are now?

Remember, a king has rules. A kingdom has boundaries. Willingly forfeiting rights and freedoms can give rise to complex and possibly unpleasant issues. Besides, what is the king like? Can he be trusted? What is the purpose of his kingdom?

The Desire for Independence

Most of us grow up longing for the day when we achieve independence. Siblings proclaim defiantly to one another, "You are not my boss! I don't have to listen to you!" This battle cry reveals the eager anticipation of someday becoming captain of our own ship. Whether in education, the military, the workplace, or society in general, humanity demonstrates an overwhelming desire to be free of control. In fact, it's increasingly common for people to show a lack of respect for authority and arrogantly dismiss others' guidance. Asking someone to willingly be subjected to anyone is a hard sell.

Jesus's invitation to enter God's kingdom requires that we give up our right to independently rule our own lives. He offers to be our king and shepherd. For most people, it takes a lot of convincing to remotely consider such a proposition.

To accept Jesus's offer as good news, we first need to see why the news is in fact good. People often differ in the value they assign to news. If someone announced a 1946 Popping John tractor for sale, likely you wouldn't be interested. However, if there was a 1953 mint-condition Corvette for sale, a number of people would pay attention. Going a step further, the announcement of a 75-percent-off clothing sale could cause pandemonium among many females. Whether news is considered good depends on the interest and need of the recipient.

Jesus describes both the opportunity to enter God's kingdom and having him as shepherd as good news. However, just as most sheep don't want a shepherd or believe they need one, humanity in general doesn't get too excited about the availability of the Good Shepherd. Once again, like the use of pearls to illustrate the value of the kingdom, we need a closer look at the shepherd/sheep relationship before the value of what Jesus offers becomes evident.

Advantages of Having a Shepherd

By their very nature, sheep need a shepherd. Though I know very little about sheep, I have lots of personal experience owning cattle. I work with them for their welfare much like a shepherd would.

As a good manager of my herd, I must ensure that my cows have water and forage all year. Cows can't survive winter without hay, but given the free choice, they will eat the best grass even if it's their winter hay supply. I have fences to control where and how long the cows can eat and to keep them out of the hay fields. Fences provide life for cattle because they lack the understanding to plan ahead.

Fences also keep cattle together, which helps protect them from predators. Remaining within the boundaries of the farm puts the herd under the care of the cattleman. Left to wander, cows encounter many dangers, becoming prey to predators, parasites, and diseases. Without proper vaccinations, minerals, and the intervention of the herdsman, cattle don't fare very well on their own.

A good cattleman deworms his cows to protect against intestinal parasites and vaccinates them to prevent pinkeye, blackleg, and respiratory illnesses. However, cows stubbornly resist the idea of having a caretaker, so I must put them in a mechanical squeeze chute to care for them. No matter how good my intentions are for them, they work against me the entire time. When I work with my cattle, they often jump fences and try everything possible to resist my efforts to care for them. Some cows even go so far as attempting to harm the herdsman.

Just like Jesus is the Good Shepherd, I strive to be a good cattleman. I repeatedly repair fences the cattle tear down as they defy the limits I set for their good. There's no reasoning with them! They have no interest in being managed, and they don't appreciate my efforts. As far as they're concerned, they'd do fine without fences or a herdsman. Surely humans are smarter than cows. However, given how most people react to God as shepherd, it doesn't seem that we *are* a whole lot smarter!

God invites us to give up our right to rule our own lives and embrace our need of the Shepherd through entering his kingdom, but that is the good news that most people cannot appreciate. Even within the church, most church members have no desire to be reminded of the limits God has in place for our protection. Few are eager to be taught the deep things of how life is to be lived according to God's standard. They fail to understand that God's directives are not arbitrarily

chosen boundaries but are carefully in place to give us life.

Like my cattle, many professing Christians jump fences (God's standards for life) and resist every effort of the pastor to fulfill his role as under-shepherd. When they resist guidance, life brings them much pain and sometimes even death.

Why might the disciples have considered it good news to have Jesus as their shepherd? Why were they willing to give up their independence to enter God's kingdom? The answer is that the kingdom of God is good news to those who recognize their need and desire what the kingdom offers. It is worth everything to those who know who the King is and understand their need of his management. Family offers us another example: it often takes a lot of cuts and bruises and even some life-threatening experiences before the value of parental advice can truly be appreciated.

God's rule of our lives is for our benefit. As our shepherd, he provides fences (limits and laws) to keep us healthy and safe. God takes care of us by preparing us for winter—the tough times—and standing in the gap against predators and other agents of harm, including demonic forces. God's fences and careful management of our lives is a testimony of his great love for us and his desire that we enjoy the fullness of life.

In Need of Shepherding

A few years ago, my wife and I were working at a home for boys. One boy and his brother had arrived after spending several months living on their own. They had become involved in drugs, both for self-gratification and as a livelihood. Lacking the sound judgment needed to make good choices, they had entered an adult world of crime and pleasure.

This boy, who was sixteen years old at the time, rode with me to town to buy something he wanted. On that trip, he mentioned that he really liked me. I told him it was because he had been able to con me into taking him to town. He said, "No, I like you because you are the one who makes us do what we are supposed to do."

In his new life with us, he was earning money by the sweat of his brow and the strength of his back. This gave him great satisfaction. The

rules governing his new living arrangement demanded mutual respect and care for one another, proper language, and appropriate regard for those in leadership. Because he was learning to follow these rules, he could lie down at night feeling good about himself. This was in great contrast to the fear, greed, and selfishness associated with his former life in the world of drugs and crime.

Because of the difference we made in his life, this boy gained a very positive outlook on who he was becoming. He appreciated the person who made him do what helped him feel good about himself. He was willing to give up his right to rule and submit to the leadership of another who had his best interests at heart and would help him do what was right by enforcing guidelines and boundaries that, in the end, would give him a future.

SUBMISSION TO THE SHEPHERD

In the same way, the kingdom of God is good news to those ready and willing to give up their right to rule and surrender themselves to the Good Shepherd. These people acknowledge that God is their Maker and that he rightfully deserves their submission as they live in his world.

Those of us who have made the decision to enter the kingdom know we aren't strong enough to fight against all that could harm us. Like the youth from the boys' home, we are content to receive guidance. We know we're not smart enough to anticipate and handle all life can bring. Through the choice to enter God's kingdom, we state unapologetically our need and desire for God as our shepherd and the appropriateness of submitting to our Creator.

Jesus requires that we become like children in order to enter the kingdom. This involves a high level of trust, but also a desire to be parented. Many very young children ask their parents if they will ever have to move out. Later, as they get older, they want to know how soon they can go. When they're mature, they come to the Father above saying, "Can I come back home? I need you as Father in my life."

The disciples knew the King, and they were certainly smarter than cows! They recognized their need for fences and a shepherd, so they

entered God's kingdom willingly, desiring to live under God's rule. They were convinced that by submitting to God, they would be protected from things that could harm them and led to things that would give them life. The disciples knew that submission is the only appropriate response to the source and Creator of life.

If Cows Could Talk

For cows, having someone to watch over them has great benefits. On the other side of the spectrum are those who farm by the survival-of-the-fittest program: They drop the cows off in a field to fend for themselves. No minerals or vaccinations are provided. No one cares for their injuries or provides assistance when they have trouble giving birth. The grass is not managed, and the weeds are not controlled. The rule of living is "do the best you can with what you have."

If cows could talk, they'd tell new cows arriving at my farm that the herdsman is faithful to take care of them. "We don't always like it, and we constantly resist him, but in the end he makes us do what we are supposed to do. To the best of his ability, we always have water and food regardless of the weather. He doesn't beat us or use electric cattle prods. Instead, he works gently with our unwillingness to be managed. He won't neglect us, but constantly tries to be aware of anything out of the ordinary. Be thankful you'll be managed by someone committed to your welfare."

Cows can't talk, but we can. Those of us who have seized the opportunity of the kingdom say that living within the realm of God's rule is the chance of a lifetime. No price is too high. It is a call to a life-giving relationship with the One who loves us and is committed to the welfare of our lives.

Trust

As a good cattleman, I practice the grass-management technique of cross-pasturing. Using this technique, I control the number of days my cows are allowed to graze in a particular field before I move them to another. Proper rotation allows grasses to recover from grazing and consequently produce more volume. My cows have learned that when I ask them to

move, they are going to a better field where there is plenty of fresh grass to eat. I don't have to drive them with horses, dogs, and four-wheelers. I just step into the field and call. They lift their heads in response to the first call, and by the second call they come running to follow me wherever I go. They've learned to trust that where I'm taking them is a better place.

However, calves are a different story. Some may have just been born in the field, and consequently they have no experience with me as the herdsman. My wife and our cattle dog have the job of bringing up the rear by keeping the calves with the group. By the second or third move, calves learn to trust the value of these transitions.

If cows can learn to trust me, perhaps there's hope that we can learn to trust the Good Shepherd. Maybe we can even learn to accept the fences he has put in place to give us life. Over time, my cows have come to know who I am and have a small understanding of what I can do for them. Fortunately, God is patient with us. His desire is for us to learn to trust him.

My cattle know my voice. When I step into a field, they all look my way, waiting to see if I will call. It is a beautiful picture of the role God desires to have in our lives. God does not seek to be king so he can have the fun of ruling us. Rather, out of his nature of love, God desires to give us what is good. His role as shepherd is to protect us from harm and lead us to life. Jesus says, "My sheep listen to my voice; I know them, and they follow me" (John 10:27).

Recently, when I was leading my cows to another pasture, my neighbor called for his brother to come watch my cows following me like a "pied piper." Most people assume the only way cows can be moved is to drive them against their will. In the past, this man had seen cattle being driven, but not led. The sight struck him with amazement.

DRIVEN OR LED?

Within the realm of what is called Christianity, we seldom see those who follow the voice of the Shepherd. Separating their faith from their day-to-day lives, professing Christians are often driven by fear, selfish desires,

and religious pride—but not by the voice of God. In today's popular health, wealth, and prosperity movement, many are driven by the promise of material gain through spirituality rather than by a desire to submit to the Shepherd. It is my prayer that someday people will call for their neighbors to come and see when they observe Christians who are led by God rather than driven by their selfish interests.

Spending time with the Shepherd for the purpose of knowing his voice is essential for life in the kingdom of God. Jesus describes this relationship of sheep and shepherd in the book of John: "The watchman opens the gate for him, and the sheep listen to his voice. He calls his own sheep by name and leads them out. When he has brought out all his own, he goes on ahead of them, and his sheep follow him because they know his voice" (John 10:3–4).

Those who truly follow the voice of the Shepherd can be seen living life as Jesus did. Otherwise, we show that we are fooling ourselves about having relationship with him. In Matthew 7, Jesus made it clear that it isn't those who just say, "Lord, Lord," who will enter the kingdom. Instead, it's people who do the Father's will. According to Matthew 7:22–23, those who end up being rejected by Jesus protest that they prophesied, cast out demons, and did mighty works in his name. Yet Jesus says, "I never knew you." This means that as sheep, they neither knew nor responded to him as shepherd.

Unexpected Disappointment

The expanded version of Jesus's message to the religious people in Matthew 7 might have gone like this: "I never knew you. You never took time to know my voice. I stepped into the field of your life, and you ignored me. I called to you, and you did not respond. You lived as captain of your ship without acknowledging you needed me. You didn't admit you were in need of change or under the obligation to live according to my standards. You didn't see that the fences were there for your own good or respect their limits. You were unwilling to give up your personal right to rule your own life."

Those who only want to avoid hell and get in on heaven have no

desire to submit to God or live with him as shepherd. They may be sadly surprised and disappointed, like the group Jesus described in Matthew 7. People who want to go to heaven without yielding to God as shepherd are seeking something Jesus wasn't offering. They are similar to the Jews who wanted a political kingdom rather than the kingdom of God. What Jesus offered was different—and vastly more valuable.

INVITATION TO LIFE

Seeing the value—the good news—of choosing God as king and shepherd separates the few from the many. Only when God is seen as supreme in value and allowed to be supreme in authority do we enjoy the full benefits of life in his kingdom. God is strong enough to control us against our will, but he won't. As Psalm 23 suggests, he leads to life those who see him as the fulfillment of all they need.

> The LORD is my shepherd, I shall not be in want. He makes me lie down in green pastures, he leads me beside quiet waters, he restores my soul. He guides me in paths of righteousness for his name's sake. Even though I walk through the valley of the shadow of death, I will fear no evil, for you are with me; your rod and your staff, they comfort me. You prepare a table before me in the presence of my enemies. You anoint my head with oil; my cup overflows. Surely goodness and love will follow me all the days of my life, and I will dwell in the house of the LORD forever. (Psalm 23)

In the end, Jesus's invitation to enter God's kingdom is not an oxymoron. Having God as your shepherd through life in his kingdom is truly good news. Your decision to enter the small gate is based on willingly taking the opportunity to live under the rule of God. This decision is not a "have to" but rather a "want to." Your king maintains boundaries, but they are for your good. Refusing God's offer in arrogance and independence has grave consequences.

A shepherd not only maintains boundaries but works faithfully to

help with injuries or intervene in illnesses or difficulties at lambing time. In order to assure the best results possible for the flock, the shepherd is constantly looking ahead to make available clean water and protein-rich grasses for the sheep so that they can thrive. In a similar way, as shepherd in our lives, God has great desires that we might thrive in his kingdom. Jeremiah 29:11 states: "'For I know the plans I have for you,' declares the LORD, 'plans to prosper you and not to harm you, plan to give you a hope and a future.'"

God rightfully deserves our submission to him as we live in his world. He could demand and enforce submission, but he won't. He delights when we acknowledge that we need his shepherding. By trusting him with our lives, each of us can establish a personal relationship with God that will revolutionize our existence. Through recognizing that God is supreme in value and authority, we can thrive within the life-giving boundaries he sets in his kingdom.

REFLECTING ON CHAPTER 2

What are some of the fences that God puts in our lives? How are these fences life-giving?

In what ways are you living life to the fullest because Jesus is your shepherd?

Those who want to avoid hell and get in on heaven with no desire to submit to God as shepherd will be sadly surprised in the end because they are seeking something Jesus is not offering. What more is required?

God rightfully deserves our submission and could force us to respond positively to him. Instead, by offering us the opportunity to trust him as our shepherd, he establishes a relationship that can revolutionize our lives. What is required to make this relationship a reality in your life?

Chapter Three

Knowing About God

LIKE MANY OTHER PEOPLE who grew up in church, I knew *about* God. Accounts of what God did in the past were very familiar. I also was well aware of Jesus, who lived and died to gain salvation for everyone. It appeared that God had finished what needed to be accomplished, and his personal interaction with humanity was no longer needed.

To my mind, with the Bible available to tell us about God and how to get to heaven through Jesus, people needed only to believe what they read. My awareness of God was similar to my knowledge of the events which led to the founding of America. I placed them on an equal footing, believing the facts I read about God and the founding of America simply to be true.

CHANGE

However, after my treetop experiences, my reading about God changed. Now, when reading the Scriptures, something similar to what happened in the treetop began to happen inside of me. Instead of being distant and unfamiliar, the historical events of the Bible began to take on life. Scriptural accounts began to touch me, validated by my own encounters with God. I was no longer just reading about God, but rather experiencing him in pages that had once conveyed only historical facts. It was as if I'd moved from viewing photos to watching a movie, and from being in the audience to personally interacting with what was happening.

Like most people, I don't have that level of experience every time I

open the Book. Just as it is in life, there are varying degrees in the ways God touches us. There are also surprises, because God is not predictable when it comes to how and when he breaks through to us. We can encounter God while looking at a beautiful sunset, listening to the birds sing, gazing at the canopy of the stars, or deeply examining a particular passage of Scripture.

In addition to these kinds of quiet moments, God can also meet us in times of crisis, moments of death, and at other times and ways quite unexpected. C.S. Lewis spoke of contact with God often being oblique—not straight on but from the side and at times and ways not planned for.

Jeremiah provides an example of how an encounter with God can even occur in unusual circumstances. Jeremiah had been rejected for his preaching, beaten, imprisoned, and laughed at, so he decided to quit. He found out that it wasn't going to be that easy. "But if I say, 'I will not mention him or speak any more in his name,' his word is in my heart like a fire, a fire shut up in my bones. I am weary of holding it in; indeed, I cannot" (Jeremiah 20:9). God's approach came to Jeremiah even when he was in no mood to receive it.

We cannot orchestrate the time or place for God's activity. God is the one who takes the initiative. "I revealed myself to those who did not ask for me; I was found by those who did not seek me. To a nation that did not call on my name, I said, 'Here am I, here am I'" (Isaiah 65:1). When God presents himself to us, we can respond or ignore his initiative.

The Faith Reality

By personal response to God's self-revelation, we can move from believers in history to people with experience. This shift is what the Scriptures call faith.

Faith is more than believing the truth of history. Hebrews 11:1 says, "Now faith is being sure of what we hope for and certain of what we do not see." The RSV translates it this way: "Now faith is the assurance of things hoped for, the conviction of things not seen." The original Greek words give this meaning: faith is the reality behind the object of faith (*hypostasis*) and the demonstration or proof of the things not seen (*elegchos*).

Faith is more than intellectual assent to propositions about God. In John 3, when Nicodemus asked Jesus about eternal life, he was told that he needed to be born again. He was not given a list of statements about God to memorize but rather was told that a spiritual event from God must happen to him.

Peter's declaration of Jesus as the Messiah was on the basis of a personal experience of God's self-revelation to him. As the later verses of Matthew 16 indicate, Peter still had a lot to learn. A one-time encounter with God is far from exhaustive in giving complete understanding. However, for Peter, there was a big difference between having truth validated by God and simply agreeing with the collective opinion of others.

As an example that God requires personal connection with him rather than empty belief, Isaiah writes, "The LORD says, 'These people come near to me with their mouth and honor me with their lips, but their hearts are far from me. Their worship of me is made up only of rules taught by men'" (Isaiah 29:13). The RSV translates the second part of this verse as, "their fear of me is a commandment of men learned by rote." Belief based on what others say without a personal heart connection with God is empty and does not achieve God's desire for us.

The book of Acts tells of the apostle Paul being in Ephesus and some Jews observing him using the power of Jesus's name to cast out demons. They believed that there was power in Jesus's name, but they did not have a faith experience with Jesus. These Jews attempted an exorcism by the name of Jesus whom Paul preached.

> The evil spirit answered them, "Jesus I know, and I know about Paul, but who are you?" Then the man who had the evil spirit jumped on them and overpowered them all. He gave them such a beating that they ran out of the house naked and bleeding. (Acts 19:15–16)

These men failed to realize that it is only through personal relationship with Jesus that there is power through his name.

The requirement of knowing God rather than just knowing about him is expressed vividly in the book of Jeremiah.

"The time is coming," declares the LORD, "When I will make a new covenant with the house of Israel and with the house of Judah. This is the covenant I will make with the house of Israel after that time," declares the LORD. "I will put my law in their minds and write it on their hearts. I will be their God, and they will be my people. No longer will a man teach his neighbor or a man his brother, saying, 'Know the LORD,' because they will all know me, from the least of them to the greatest," declares the LORD. (Jeremiah 31:31, 33–34).

Everyone must be sure that he or she has a connection with God that is more than just knowing about him. Jesus echoes the importance of this distinction when he says to those professing relationship with him, "I never knew you. Away from me, you evildoers!" (Matthew 7:23).

God works with us in a variety of ways so that we can know him rather than just know about him. In a general way, he left his stamp on the world he created. "For since the creation of the world God's invisible qualities—his eternal power and divine nature—have been clearly seen, being understood from what has been made, so that men are without excuse" (Romans 1:20). Supremely, God was in Jesus as the ultimate self-revelation of who he is and his desire for his creation. Jesus's teachings, then, are not based on the opinion of men or religious projections, but are truth statements emerging out of his unity with the Father. If we respond to God's prompting by being spiritually born again, the means is established for each of us to have an intimate personal relationship in knowing God.

The movement from the English expression "believe" to the biblical expression "faith" is transformational. Unfortunately, many never make this essential transition from belief to faith. Without faith, we are left with intellectual acceptance of facts rather than a supernatural experience of God that motivates and transforms us. Our experience of God—not our

intellectual acceptance of God—is the driving force for our relationship with him.

A Welcoming Father

To help others see God more clearly, Jesus told the parable of the prodigal son. In this story, the man's son took his inheritance and wasted it. In a destitute state, the son returned home seeking to be a servant in his father's house.

When he was almost home, his father ran to meet him. The exchange between father and son was priceless. As the son began to confess to his father about sinning against heaven and against him and feeling unworthy to be called his son, the father called for the servants to let the party begin!

The story centers on the revealed heart and constant hope the father had for his son. The father's willing forgiveness and compassion for his son mirrors God's love for us. The wayward son's amazed surprise and comfort in his father's embrace is equally God's desire for us. Both through his teaching and personal life example, Jesus sought to give us a glimpse of the heavenly Father.

The Truck or the Field?

In our culture, many sports fans refer to famous male athletes as "The Man," the person at the apex of his field and the measure of what everyone should imitate. When we are touched by God in life experiences and through reading the Scriptures, there should be no question as to who The Man is.

Last summer, my eight-year-old grandson Nathanael demonstrated his desire to be The Man. He tied one end of a piece of rope to an old uprooted tree stump and tied the other end to his waist. Then he ran up and down the driveway dragging the stump behind him.

His sister, Caraline, wondered what could have compelled him to do such a thing. Their conversation went something like this: "Excuse me, sir," said Caraline, sounding like a reporter. "What exactly are you doing?" She was equipped with a mock microphone and a clipboard to take notes.

"I'm in training," said Nathanael, out of breath.

As if interviewing a celebrated athlete, Caraline nodded and asked, "What are you conditioning yourself to do?"

"I want to be able to pick up a square bale of hay," was the reply.

At my farm, we use square bales to store hay for the winter. Each weighs approximately forty to fifty pounds. A bale of hay is a considerable load for an eight-year-old. That summer, Nathanael had ridden in the truck while we were gathering the hay from the field and storing it in the barn. He had experienced hay hauling as the boy in the truck, but what he wanted was to be the man in the field.

Enjoying the comforts of a cattleman's dual-wheel, four-door, one-ton truck with leather seats, air-conditioning, stereo, snacks, and drinks close at hand is not a bad ride. Yet the boy in the truck looks at the man in the field and wants to do whatever is necessary to make that transition.

This year, when it was time to haul hay, Nathanael moved from the truck to the field. It was a typical Tennessee summer day. The sun was beating down at ninety-five degrees, and there was a mixture of hay and dust in the air as we worked. With all he had, he began picking up bales of hay, barely able to make them clear the ground. He would stagger as he made his way to the wagon. Later, in the heat and dust of the barn, he pulled the bales to me as we pitched them up higher to be stacked.

Struggling against what for him were enormous weights, Nathanael did not quit or complain. He refused all offers to take a break and ride in the truck. He stayed with us for the duration of the day as the man in the field.

Turning Point

Long before he helped with haying, Nathanael had envisioned what he wanted, set a goal, and prepared diligently so he could make the transition from the spectator comforts of the truck. If he were told he could ride in the truck next year, he'd refuse. If he were told it was too hard a job for him, he'd say, "I love my papaw, and there is nothing better than being with him on the farm doing whatever he is doing." The boy had reached a turning point. "It's not work," he'd say, "it's farming."

Like my Nathanael watching men in the field, we need to look at Jesus and say, "That's the One I want to be like." When Jesus offered God's kingdom to those around him, some were deeply stirred and others weren't. Unless you allow God's initiative of reaching out to you to stir deeply within you, no amount of influence will compel you to enter his kingdom.

Sadly, some read the Scriptures and all they see is history. Others read the same Scriptures and experience the magnificence of God. Some take the time to investigate, while others don't.

Reluctant Christians who can't wait for church to be over and wandering Christians who need to be constantly bumped back on track need to investigate why they seem to lack this driving desire to know God more fully. Only when you see God as supreme in value and allow him to be supreme in authority as your shepherd will you be able to experience him fully and know the joys of life in his kingdom.

EMPTY BELIEF VS SAVING FAITH

The tendency to reduce Christianity to simply "believing in God" moved later New Testament writers to address what they referred to as "empty belief" and "dead faith" as opposed to "saving faith." James addresses this in his book. "What good is it, my brothers, if a man claims to have faith but has no deeds? Can such faith save him? You believe that there is one God. Good! Even the demons believe that—and shudder" (James 2: 14, 19). There is a major difference between just believing in God and living in a relationship of trust with him as your shepherd.

For James, faith that isn't accompanied by action is dead. This means that there's more to faith than what we believe. What we believe must affect who we are and how we live. Saving faith is the result of personal connection with God as shepherd and our willingness to live with him as our king. Saving faith is expressed in seeing God as the supreme goal of life and consequently letting nothing stand in our way of fully responding to him.

A word of caution is necessary at this point. Establishing a relationship with God is far from any other experience in life. Relationship with

God comes through a lot of trial and error. A momentary decision to open the door to God does not always lead to an experience with him right away or in a major, earth-shattering way. Sometimes we have to stick with our pursuit even when it seems fruitless. The Scripture passages we have quoted earlier use phrases like "diligent search" and "seeking God with all your heart" as indicative of what yields results.

Paul told Timothy, "No one serving as a soldier gets involved in civilian affairs—he wants to please his commanding officer. Similarly, if anyone competes as an athlete, he does not receive the victor's crown unless he competes according to the rules. The hardworking farmer should be the first to receive a share of the crops. Reflect on what I am saying, for the Lord will give you insight into all this" (2 Timothy 2:4–7). Paul's point is that dedicated effort will be rewarded. The soldier wants to please his officer above all else, the athlete trains hard and plays within the rules before taking the victor's stand, and the farmer works over a long season before sharing in the harvest.

THE TRUE FOLLOWER

It's amazing to hear people say they plan on going to heaven when they die, and yet these same individuals do not respect God or live their lives as an extension of relationship to him. It would be reasonable to question how they will be satisfied living eternally in a place that is the opposite of all they have known and done in this life. Respect for God and living in relationship with him is what separates true followers of Jesus from professed followers. Those thinking that all is well as long as they just believe there is a God will be surprised at how things turn out in the end.

The Old Testament story of Jacob provides an example of how a response to God can radically change one's life. Jacob had stopped for the night as he fled from his brother, who was intending to kill him. Jacob had a dream of angels ascending and descending from heaven to earth. God stood above the ladder and announced a blessing upon his life.

When Jacob awoke from his sleep, he thought, "Surely the LORD is in this place, and I was not aware of it." He was afraid and

said, "How awesome is this place! This is none other than the house of God; this is the gate of heaven." (Genesis 28:16–17)

We, too, are to discover that God is in this place. Even though we may not be aware of it, this is the gate to heaven. What we do while living here determines whether we make it through the gateway to heaven. Jacob's discovery transformed his life, and as a consequence, he lived out the rest of his years seeking to fulfill God's desire for him. His dream gave him a totally new perspective about life. Attentiveness to God can have the same effect for us.

COMPARATIVE SALVATION

Many people cannot understand the commitment that some give to the spiritual pursuit of God. They fail to understand that relationship with God is the core meaning of our existence. Many believe that in the end, all that matters is that one believes there is a God and lives a morally decent life.

In essence, such thinking expects God to support what I call comparative salvation. Compared to others, I'm not that bad. The concept of comparative salvation promotes the idea that God will line folks up from the worst to the best and then draw a line somewhere to separate those who make it and those who don't. A host of people are counting on comparative salvation as the standard of judgment. As long as I am decent and better than most, that's all it takes.

Being a little better than others is a far cry from the relationship that God wants with us! God's desire is for a relationship based on a personal heart connection that affects who we are and how we live. This kind of relationship far exceeds the empty belief of just knowing about God.

Comparative salvation is not acceptable to God because it does not give life. Just being good and more righteous than others does not bring life. Jesus says, "Now this is eternal life: that they may know you, the only true God, and Jesus Christ, whom you have sent" (John 17:3). Knowing *about* God and being a little better than others is not having a

personal experience *of* God that gives us life and fulfills the meaning of our existence.

Faith is more than believing the truth of history. It's experiencing the reality behind the object of faith—a supernatural encounter with God. How have your life experiences and study of the Scriptures helped you participate in a journey of continuous discovery of God?

Not everyone who believes in God is experiencing relationship with him. In what ways is it evident that someone is walking with him? Is there evidence of time spent with him in your life?

The busyness of our daily life continuously interrupts and interferes with our spiritual quests. What are these interruptions and interferences like for you? What disciplines, lifestyles, friendships, associations, and habits help you keep the pressures of life and the voices of the world from disrupting and blocking your personal pursuit of God?

Chapter Four

The Apple Doesn't Fall Far from the Tree

THE LOOK OF EXCITEMENT on Nathanael's face was priceless as he grabbed his first bale of hay and started toward the wagon. His deep longing to join the men in the field had been realized! No amount of being hot, tired, and sweaty could take away the immense satisfaction he felt at no longer being the boy in the truck.

My grandson had a reachable goal. In response to his desire, he took action to prepare himself for the transition. Like the pearl merchant in Jesus's parable, Nathanael was driven by such joy that no price was too high in order for him to reach his goal.

NEW PROVISIONS

Like Nathanael's ambition, our desire to enter the kingdom depends upon seeing something of value there. However, unlike Nathanael's reachable goal, life in the kingdom of God involves things outside our normal capacity. When God is part of the equation, one should assume that it means stepping outside of the ordinary.

Unless God makes entrance into his kingdom possible, no amount of training or discipline will gain us entry. The opportunity to enter exists only because Jesus gave his life to remove the sin barrier that separates us from God. And once we have entered, the goals and purposes of God's kingdom cannot be accomplished by the strength of our drive and dedication.

Jesus explained to Nicodemus that being born again is one of the

necessary experiences for entrance into God's kingdom. "How can a man be born when he is old?" Nicodemus wondered in John 3:4. "Surely he cannot enter the second time into his mother's womb to be born!"

Jesus's use of birth as a metaphor to represent the experience of entering the kingdom provokes many questions. Even trying to apply his metaphor spiritually rather than physically (as in Nicodemus's objection) does not make everything clear.

Being spiritually born again is the start of a new level of existence with God. It takes time and discipline to learn how God's Spirit works in our lives. Jesus's additional teaching as recorded in John's gospel fleshes out more details of how Spirit-life works. The parables Jesus gives of the Good Shepherd and the vine and branch are especially helpful in describing this new dimension of life with God.

When Jesus spoke of being born again, he was describing a supernatural event. Because this experience is supernatural, explaining it is difficult. However, Jesus's use of the birth analogy does give us a reference point for understanding what he's saying. Consider these facts about birth. The union of our parents accounts for our natural birth; therefore, birth is not a product of our own action. There's also a genetic inheritance that we receive through birth that shapes us. The bond between parent and child is powerful when it works as it should. All of these things lead us to the truth of this analogy.

A Supernatural Happening

The special connection between parent and child provides a good parallel of what God does in us as we enter his kingdom. This supernatural and spiritual "birthing" is accomplished by our heavenly Father in response to our faith in him and our desire to enter his kingdom. This spiritual birthing event is God's way of giving us what we need. Being born from above is an event of regeneration and connection with God as our Father.

The birth analogy makes it clear that entering God's kingdom is not just a new way to believe or the acceptance of new religious rituals, but rather the experience of becoming a new creation. Paul describes it this

way: "Therefore, if anyone is in Christ, he is a new creation; the old has gone, the new has come!" (2 Corinthians 5:17). Paul admonishes some in the Corinthian church for not expressing the new way of life that connection with God should bring. In 1 Corinthians 3:3b, Paul asks, "Are you not acting like mere men?" His challenge implies that, as spiritual men, they should not behave in a worldly fashion but rather be empowered by the Spirit for a new way of living.

BEHAVIORAL INFLUENCE

In natural birth, we receive the powerful force of a genetic inheritance from our parents. By living with them, we are exposed to their behavioral influences as well. The genetic connection with our parents, combined with living with them during the formative years of our lives, is a powerful influence that shapes who we are.

Jesus states that the powerful force of behavioral influence is part of life in the kingdom. "If anyone loves me, he will obey my teaching. My Father will love him, and we will come to him and make our home with him" (John 14:23).

The fact of God's making his home with us is just as difficult to understand as Jesus's statement of the need to be born again. The point becomes vivid when we consider the difference between visiting someone and living with them. When we visit someone, we make contact with them occasionally. By making his home with us, Jesus is saying that God is available to us continually. Constant versus occasional interaction with God is possible. When we learn to live by this principle, God will have a powerful influence on our lives.

Children are usually very careful about what they do when their parents are around. Outside of their parents' view, many children show a different response to life. In a similar way, sensitivity to the presence of God can impact our lives greatly. However, living so we're aware of God's presence requires the spiritual discipline of attentiveness. Remember, God's gentle prodding can be ignored, drowned out by the noise of life, and even rejected.

There are many ways we can know that God is making his home

with us. For instance, have you ever felt that you were in a larger-than-life moment when viewing a sunset or the magnificence of a waterfall? In a similar way, have you ever been reading the Scriptures and experienced an increasing awareness of God? In moments when you have time to meditate, have you ever felt God's presence break into your thought world in a very impacting way? Once these unique moments with God occur, we need to stay focused and not shut off what is happening. Even after these larger-than-life moments, it is important to reflect on what happened. In this way we can glean all that God intended from such encounters.

Our culture of stress and fast-paced living makes maintaining an awareness of God difficult. Yet, when we are driven by an inward desire to be attentive to God's promptings, we allow the power of his presence to become life-changing.

THE APPLE AND THE TREE

You may have heard the saying that the apple doesn't fall far from the tree. If you stumble upon an apple, it doesn't take much searching to determine where it came from. People are not much different. All of us have observed the physical and behavioral characteristics of others that were easily traced back to their family of origin.

There is a whole science in the cattle industry that allows the cattle-man to predict a host of desirable outcomes with his herd. We want calves to be small at birth for calving ease for both calf and mother. We want to know that even though they start out small, the calves will grow quickly. We're also concerned that the females will feed their calves well and have good overall maternal qualities. We even have genetic predictions that indicate the size of the rib eye and the marbling quality of the meat we sell. The power of genetic inheritance has been monitored and used in the cattle industry for a very long time. The fact that the apple doesn't fall very far from the tree is a welcomed and valued principle on the farm!

How does this apply to us spiritually? In spiritual rebirth, we don't get a new set of chromosomes. What happens to us is not natural, but

spiritual. Jesus's metaphor of being born again tells us that a connection is made with God *as our Father* that affects us.

When it comes to sports, knowing the physical characteristics of my lineage is a great predictor of my potential to play professionally. In a similar way, knowing that my heavenly Father is the God of love and the Creator of the universe indicates that I have the potential to rise above the crazy obsessions of this world.

It is clear that the apostle Paul understood that a spiritual connection with Jesus is to have an effect on who we are:

> If you have any encouragement from being united with Christ, if any comfort from his love, if any fellowship with the Spirit, if any tenderness and compassion, then make my joy complete by being like-minded, having the same love, being one in spirit and purpose. Do nothing out of selfish ambition or vain conceit, but in humility consider others better than yourselves. Each of you should look not only to your own interests, but also to the interests of others. Your attitude should be the same as that of Christ Jesus. (Philippians 2:1–5)

God's spiritual connection with us through the new birth is more powerful than a new set of chromosomes! It's a bond not easily defined with natural concepts. It is a life-changing and life-giving power.

Another apple saying is that one bad apple ruins the whole barrel. Folks storing apples in a barrel for the winter learn quickly what happens when a bad apple is in close proximity to the rest. Sociologists, parents, and people in general are acutely aware of the power of behavioral influences. So are cattlemen. A wild and uncontrollable cow is soon removed from the farm before her behavior has a negative effect on the rest of the herd. Proverbs 13:20 offers a strong statement concerning behavioral influences: "He who walks with the wise grows wise, but a companion of fools suffers harm."

New birth and behavioral influences are the means greater than ourselves needed for our new way of life. Being born from above and having

the Father living in us are essential to life in God's kingdom. They are not options. They are necessary. We won't get to where God intends us to go without them.

THE GATE IS TOO SMALL

For some, these supernatural events of new birth and God living in us make the gate to God's kingdom too difficult to enter. Such spiritual transactions have no place in their natural way of thinking. Many think a simpler, more rational approach to God is all that is needed. For them, speaking of interacting spiritually with God takes things too far.

The concept of comparative salvation described in the previous chapter is an example of what many would consider a more reasonable response when it comes to God. But they could not be more wrong. Knowing God personally through a heart connection, being spiritually changed by his Spirit, following him as shepherd, and loving him more than life is not being "obsessive," but rather giving to our Creator the appropriate response he deserves.

Certainly, what God has made available through Jesus is mind-blowing! As I stated earlier, these are supernatural events and therefore are not easily incorporated into our normal approach to life. This is a hurdle we all must negotiate. However, by further study and additional experiences of responding to God's prompting, we can progressively understand and embrace these concepts more fully.

The wonder of our faith is that the sovereign Lord of the universe wants to make a personal connection with us. It would be foolish to think that such an experience with God is a no-brainer like learning to ride a bicycle. The fact that supernatural events accompany such an encounter with God should not surprise us—beginning with new birth and expanding into a lifestyle of walking with God.

In Jesus's explanation to Nicodemus, he described new birth as being like the wind. We don't know where it's coming from or where it goes, but we can certainly tell when it's blowing. According to Jesus, not having detailed answers to all of our questions should not prevent us from raising our sail in response to God's movement on our lives.

A Warning

The analogy that the apple doesn't fall far from the tree gives us hope that the change we desire to see in ourselves will come. It's also a warning. When others look at our lives, they shouldn't have to look very far to recognize our Father. Jesus says, "In the same way, let your light shine before men, that they may see your good deeds and praise your Father in heaven" (Matthew 5:16).

Professing Christians who fail to have any family resemblance must question whether they have just said, "Lord, Lord," or have truly been born again with God living within them. The New Testament unapologetically demands that life with God change us. "Whoever claims to live in him must walk as Jesus did" (1 John 2:6).

Family of Believers

Another way God shapes our behavior is captured in the following passage of Scripture:

> Then Jesus' mother and brothers arrived. Standing outside, they sent someone in to call him. A crowd was sitting around him and they told him, "Your mother and brothers are outside looking for you."
>
> "Who are my mother and my brothers?" he asked. Then he looked at those seated in a circle around him and said, "Here are my mother and my brothers! Whoever does God's will is my brother and sister and mother." (Mark 3:31–35)

Not only does each person who enters the kingdom experience new birth and the indwelling of God, but we together become a family of believers by being connected to the same spiritual Father. In natural families, older siblings can be a curse or a blessing. Younger siblings learn to do a lot of things earlier with the influence of older brothers and sisters. In the spiritual realm, older and more mature Christian siblings can be role models who help us learn to live by our new empowerment. Having someone to lean on who's a little further down the road is a tremendous

asset. However, today's spirit of independence can separate Christians from this valuable, shaping tool of being part of a family of believers, so it may take persistence to find a good, supportive friend or mentor. When we take our relationship with God seriously, we can sense his presence in others, and it will draw us to share a relationship with them.

Some Christians say that the woods or the lake are their sanctuary, and they have no need for church. Certainly God can be found in these places, but when you make an outdoors experience a substitute for the family of believers, there are some serious consequences. John says, "We know that we have passed from death into life, because we love our brothers. Anyone who does not love remains in death. . . . This is how we know what love is: Jesus Christ laid down his life for us. And we ought to lay down our lives for our brothers" (1 John 3:14, 16).

It's hard to imagine how someone can lay down his life for others while sitting alone in the woods or boating across a lake. Kingdom followers bond immediately with each other as they sense the common parentage of God the Father. Loving the family of God is evidence of being born of God (1 John 4).

In a natural family, members usually exhibit a variety of giftedness. Recently, our niece brought her husband to our home for my wife and I to meet. He's a mechanic, so I quickly seized the opportunity to discuss an ongoing mechanical issue I was having with my tractor. It was only taking me about thirty minutes to fix the problem, but breakdowns were occurring in the middle of other tasks. As we say on the farm, "It doesn't break down unless you're using it." Having five guys sitting on a hay wagon watching me twist bolts for thirty minutes was not pleasant or cost-effective. Joe researched the problem and gave me a fix that only takes thirty seconds. What a change! This family member's skills sure made life easier for me.

It's the same in the family of believers. God gifts each of us differently, and some types of spiritual growth can only be achieved as we're involved with God's family. The God of love is best experienced through relationships of love and commitment with each other. Paul, using the analogy of a body with its many parts, says, "From him the whole body, joined

and held together by every supporting ligament, grows and builds itself up in love, as each part does its work" (Ephesians 4:16). God's design for the interconnection of his spiritual family is similar to the miraculous way the parts of our bodies work together to sustain life. The value of being part of a committed family of believers is hard for many to appreciate. However, with God inspiring and empowering us, God's family is one of the richest treasures of his kingdom.

THE WAY TO LIFE

Life in the kingdom of God is about changing us, and our ability to change has been given by God. Once again, some say they don't mind believing in God to escape hell and gain a place in heaven, but all of this born-again stuff, with the idea of God living in us and the concept of being part of God's family, takes things way too far. Yet these concepts are not optional. They work together to bring about the desired change God intends for us.

Spiritual birth from above not only allows you to live in the kingdom but also allows the King to live in you. It's the only path Jesus offered as the way to life. It is the unfathomable dimension of what it means to be in God's kingdom. The indwelling presence of God brings us the influence we need to adjust the way we live. The presence of his Spirit is the demonstration of God's commitment to be involved in our lives, effecting the changes that will bring us life.

The God of love makes all of this possible. However, your response is required. God will not force or coerce you, for that is not the way of love. The degree to which we allow God to change us is the degree to which we'll experience the fullness of life.

REFLECTING ON CHAPTER 4

How would you describe your personal experience of larger-than-life moments (such as viewing the glory of a sunset, reading the Scriptures, or having God's presence break into your thought world)?

The analogy of the apple not falling far from the tree gives us hope and simultaneously warns us. Jesus called us to let our light shine so that others will praise our Father in heaven. How does this call separate true followers of Christ from false believers who only profess to believe?

For many, Christianity centers on attending church rather than life in the family of God. In what ways have you experienced the family of God as one of the greatest treasures of the kingdom? How can the Christian family be made known to our world?

Chapter Five

The Design of the Creator

IF YOU WERE FACED with the responsibility of feeding all the people, plants, and animals living in our world, how would you do it? At the most basic level, how would you meet the oxygen needs of people and animals and at the same time deal with the carbon dioxide they exhale? It's staggering to consider the amount of nourishment required and realize that the same need will repeat itself tomorrow.

Living things need energy to survive. Therefore, God placed an energy source ninety-three million miles from the earth: the sun. Plants use the carbon dioxide that animals exhale, combined with sunlight and water, to provide the oxygen and nourishment needed for animal life to exist. By any standard, photosynthesis is a marvelous design. Plants and animals are in a unique relationship where each benefits from the other.

I've always been interested in how things work. The design idea behind why something was made in a particular way fascinates me. Faced with the need to put something together to accomplish a useful purpose excites me.

I have enormous respect for God as the ultimate designer! The miracle of sight, the workings of the human body, the consistent pattern of our solar system, the ability for life to be sustained on our planet, the wonder of the cycle of life in plants and animals and the sheer beauty of our world all speak volumes about the magnificence of the One who created us. The intricate makeup of our natural world points to an ordered, intelligently planned design.

CHILDREN OF GOD

At the apex of God's creation is humanity, made in his image, with each individual having a soul. As the crowning mark of such a uniquely designed world, surely we have an important purpose in God's plan.

In John 1 we read an important summary statement which defines the goal of Jesus's mission to our world. John tells us that Jesus was the Word that was with God and was God. Life was in him, and he made all that is. The Word became flesh and came to live in our world as the true light to enlighten every man.

In spite of Jesus being the Word and coming to enlighten all men, he was rejected by many, even of his own people. "Yet to all who received him, to those who believed in his name, he gave the right to become children of God—children born not of natural descent, nor of human decision or a husband's will, but born of God" (John 1:12–13).

God's purpose for creating our world, and consequently the meaning of our existence, is captured in the mission of Jesus for us to become children of God. The magnitude of who Jesus is as the eternal Word with the Father is overwhelming. That the Word becomes flesh in order to empower all who will to become children of God is incomprehensible. God's self-involvement in our world brings a level of importance to his goal that is mind-blowing.

There are times when the grandeur of what is being said does not register with the listener. "America, the land of the free and the home of the brave" is an example. This well-known phrase acknowledges the sacrifice of many who secured the freedom we enjoy as a nation. However, unless one has served in combat, lost loved ones in war, lived under a harsh dictator, or experienced life in a war-torn nation, the price and value of freedom will not truly be appreciated.

In order to expose the enormity of God's purpose for our world, we need to take a deeper look at the concept so commonly referred to in Christianity of "getting saved." The question of whether one is saved or not for many sums up the essence of Christianity. Even Jesus speaks of having come to seek and save those who are lost (Matthew 18:11). Indeed, we need a savior and are lost without his intervention. However,

it is possible to let this part of what Jesus does obscure the larger picture of his purpose for us as described in John 1.

The lines of an old hymn of the church say, "Rescue the perishing, care for the dying, Jesus is merciful, Jesus will save." We can visualize this concept in the event of rescuing people from a ship that is going down. We could refer to those rescued as "survivors" or those who were "saved." But God's goal for us to become his children is a greater goal than just not letting us go down with the ship. Without Christ, we will certainly die—but with him we can *live*. The important point is that one leads to the other. Being saved from the penalty of death is but a consequence of God's purpose that we become his children.

In Christianity, we should not refer to ourselves as merely survivors—or those "saved"—but as children of God! When one thinks of getting saved as the essence of Christianity, wrong conclusions can be drawn. Some may look for the irreducible minimum requirement that guarantees life after death, with no regard for God's desire that we become his children. Some even ask, "Can you have Jesus as Savior without having him as Lord?" The answer is, "Who would want to?"

Jesus's invitation for us to enter the kingdom of God by being born of the Father and indwelt by his Spirit is a far cry from only looking for a way to keep from going down with the ship! The desire for a Savior without a Lord is an all-about-me transaction that does not fit what God invites us to. All of the pieces of responding spiritually to God by being born of him, choosing to yield to him as our king, and desiring to be shepherded by him as our Father are components of this parent-child relationship. Anything less does not give us life and does not complete the purpose God has for our lives.

The apostle Paul echoes God's goal that we become his children: "For you did not receive a spirit that makes you a slave again to fear, but you received the Spirit of sonship. And by him we cry, 'Abba! Father.' The Spirit himself testifies with our spirit that we are God's children" (Romans 8:15–16). If our view of God's purpose for us is to become his children, be in his family, and have him as our heavenly Father, we will not be looking for the irreducible minimum commitment, but rather be

investing our lives in pursuit of the greatest opportunity we will ever be offered—becoming a child of God!

Best Possible World?

Many question the suitableness of God's design of our world. Is this the best of possible worlds?

With the power to do things however he chose, why did God place us in this natural world? Why didn't God just speak into being what he wants us to be? Why take the risk that his plan could be followed or rejected?

In God's plan, he offers a process of love and freedom based in relationship to accomplish his goal that we become his children. One price of God's desire for such a relationship is that love cannot be forced. Freedom to love or reject God introduces the opportunity to abuse God's desire for us. God takes the risk in order to make possible a relationship based on choice, desire, and the acknowledgment of our need of him as our Father.

For God to create persons who are free from the risks inherent in personal freedom is to create helpless puppets. A being not susceptible to the risks of freedom is not capable of becoming a child of God who enjoys the love and trust involved in a meaningful relationship.

It is no small thing that God must endure the pain of observing how his creation has moved in the wrong direction. However, the end result of us becoming his children is important enough to him that he is willing to endure the pain of watching us being absorbed in our selfishness rather than living in his love. God could have made a world of pleasure and filled it with robots, but instead he created an environment that allows those who will to rise to the intention of their Creator to become his children.

Seek and Find

Just as becoming God's children opens us up to a process of spiritual development that starts with being born of God, the whole dimension of seeking and responding to God is not a one-time event, but rather an ongoing pursuit.

Acts 17 tells of Paul being in Athens, Greece. He went to the Are-

opagus, where philosophers and wisdom seekers met to discuss the meaning of life. It was said of this group that they spent their time doing nothing but talking about and listening to the latest ideas. Paul spoke with these thinkers about God's purpose for our existence. He announced to the Athenians that God's goal for humanity is that we seek for him and find him.

When Paul speaks of finding God, it's not an intellectual assessment or a one-time event he has in mind, but rather an ongoing pursuit. A few months ago, I lost my special pocketknife that had belonged to my father-in-law. I consistently kept my eyes alert to the possibility of finding it. One day, on a walk across the farm with my wife, Gale, I found my knife. It was a pleasure to once again put it in my pocket.

Finding God is not like finding my knife! God is not a finite object that, once discovered, requires no further searching. God is infinite; therefore, finding God involves an infinite search. There are numerous ways we continue our search for God. The study of the Scriptures, prayer, meditation, and reading the writings of Christians past and present are points of input into our quest. Learning to listen to the voice of the Shepherd and incorporating God's ways into how we live our lives are further ways of experiencing God and as a result enlarging our view of him.

Design Intention

Recently I was helping a friend repair a fence, and I used a special feature on my fencing tool to tighten some sagging barbed wire. My friend said, "I'm seventy years old, and I've never seen anyone use fencing pliers in that way." The one who designed the fencing tool gave it several working possibilities, but many people never use this tool fully as designed.

In a similar way, when we use a computer as though it's a typewriter, someone's design intention is cut short. When I discovered that the rule for manuscripts is one space at the end of a sentence rather than two, I was quite distressed at having to make all of those changes to what I'd already written. My friend Cathy introduced me to the find-and-replace feature in my software program, and the project was completed with the click of my mouse.

It's disappointing for anyone who designs something to see their creation not being used according to its intended purpose. I'm sure God agonizes over how people minimize the reason for our existence. When it comes to fencing pliers and computers, there's a lot to learn before these tools can function at the level of their intended design. The same is true for how we should live to fulfill God's purpose for us as his children. It is only through a lifetime pursuit and response to God that we can come close to the possibilities available to us as part of God's family.

NOW AND UNENDING

The eternal Word has entered our world to empower us to be his children. How unfathomable is that! Yet, there's more. What God intends for us in becoming his children applies now and on into an unending future.

Paul writes in Ephesians 3:10–11, "His intent was that now, through the church, the manifold wisdom of God should be made known to the rulers and authorities in the heavenly realms, according to his eternal purpose which he accomplished in Christ Jesus our Lord." We are not given full details about the identity of these rulers in the heavenly realm; however, Paul's point is that there is an influence now being accomplished by the people of God. It is an influence that we participate in, and it is part of the eternal purpose of God. As we willingly respond to God as our Father, our lives have a present usefulness to the Father.

It is exciting to consider that what God is doing in us is part of an eternal plan. Paul writes, "We are God's workmanship, created in Christ Jesus to do good works, which God prepared in advance for us to do" (Ephesians 2:10). God is not directing our lives with a plan-as-you-go approach; rather, he is using plans made before time began.

Jesus said, "Let your light shine before men, that they may see your good deeds and praise your Father in heaven" (Matthew 5:16). Paul says that we are a new creation as God's children. God is making his appeal to the world through us (2 Corinthians 5:19–20). He goes on to say, "Now to him who is able to do immeasurably more than all we ask or imagine, according to his power that is at work within us, to him be

glory in the church and in Christ Jesus throughout all generations, forever and ever! Amen!" (Ephesians 3:20–21).

FUTURE RESPONSIBILITIES

Paul's challenge that glory in the church be given to God throughout all generations forever and ever brings up an additional aspect of God's purpose for us as his children.

Jesus spoke to his disciples about future responsibilities. "I tell you the truth, at the renewal of all things, when the Son of Man sits on his glorious throne, you who have followed me will also sit on twelve thrones, judging the twelve tribes of Israel" (Matthew 19:28). Through following Jesus in this life, they were preparing to serve in the future. The same is true for you and me.

Unquestionably, Jesus understood the overall plan for our lives, and he speaks to this in one of his parables. In Matthew 25, Jesus compared the kingdom of heaven to a man going on a journey and entrusting his servants with his property. Each servant was given certain assets based on his ability to manage them. When the master returned, he expected that each servant should have increased what he had been allotted. The one who hid his portion in the ground and only had what was given to him was cast into outer darkness. Those who invested and increased what had been entrusted to them heard, "Well done, good and faithful servant! You have been faithful with a few things; I will put you in charge of many things. Come and share your Master's happiness!" (Matthew 25:23).

The servant who hid what he was given represents those who refuse the opportunity to invest themselves in God's kingdom. They do not grow spiritually and do nothing to advance God's purposes. However, those who respond to the voice of God gain a new perspective on life, even a cosmic perspective which transforms the way they live. When we choose to embrace the full dimension of new birth and God's indwelling, we are being prepared for out-of-this-world experiences.

Scripture does not give us a lot of details about the next life. We know that we will not marry, get sick, or die. There will be no night in

the eternal kingdom—life in the future is one eternal day. The next life will be different from this one in countless ways, but in one way it will be the same: those who willingly invest themselves in the will of God will continue doing in the future what they are already doing here—serving God's purpose for their lives.

WALK, DON'T RIDE

God's use of this world to prepare us for enjoyable service in the next is exciting to hear. Personally, I want to arrive well prepared for whatever my present relationship with God equips me for.

I sometimes tell people, "If I were a dog, I'd be a border collie." When Lady, my Labrador retriever, and Sada, my border collie, go with me to feed hay, the Lab finds a soft place in the hay wagon and takes a nap—but not Sada! She'd rather walk than ride. She wants to beat me to the gate so she'll be ready to make sure the cows don't get out as I come through. She's always excited about working and willing to serve.

In a similar way, having a relationship with God is walking, not riding asleep in the hay. Those who love God look forward to any chance to do whatever task serves his purpose. Life in the kingdom allows God to complete his intention for us to enjoy the fullness of life and to be prepared for responsibilities in the world to come.

A SMALL GLIMPSE

The idea of God having preestablished plans for us, in this world and not just the next one, is probably new to a lot of people. These concepts are outside their understanding of what it means to be a Christian. Believing in God and trying to be good with the hope of heaven is the limited scope of many who ascribe to Christianity. The idea of a kingdom, the will of the King, and the functional purpose of our lives now as well as into the future are concepts far removed from their consideration.

When we come to the understanding that God created the earth from a plan to fit into what was going on in heaven, our whole idea of Christianity, salvation, and the road to life turns in a different direction.

From this perspective, heaven is the ongoing realm of God that we enter to accomplish the purpose God originated when he created each of us.

There are many dimensions to a life with God. God's eternal power and divine nature are found through the many expressions of himself in the wonder of our world. Each time we respond to God's inner prompting, we're able to see him and his ways more clearly. The Bible provides a way to meet God as he speaks in unique ways to all who search its pages. Each time we follow God's commands and as a result experience fullness of life, we grow in the ability to let God show us even more of himself and his life-giving ways. To seek and find God is an exciting, life-changing, and endless journey.

God had a detailed purpose in mind when he decided to create our world. He placed us in a natural world that can be seen as an end in itself or, through faith, as a place with infinite meaning and purpose. The continual process of seeking and finding God by pursuing him diligently as his children achieves his purpose in us.

By faith we experience God's spiritual realm. When we choose to submit to God and live according to his ways, a trust relationship is established. When we mature in our faith and spiritual connection with God, God intentionally prepares us for activities now and in the life to come.

Even a small glimpse of God's plan and purpose for us should stir in us an excitement to pursue all that is available. In a way, our willingness to be shaped, recreated, and matured in spiritual abilities makes our world God's laboratory in which he works to mature us as his children. Our world is an amazing place in which God achieves his desire that Jesus become the firstborn of many brethren (Romans 8:29).

REFLECTING ON CHAPTER 5

Some think of Christianity as a heaven to gain, a hell to avoid, and a solution to the fact that we all die. What has helped you understand that God's purpose in salvation is more than this?

Just as many people cut short a computer's capabilities, how do we cut short God's intention of being involved in our lives?

Finding God involves a continual search. It is one that is never completed. Do you agree with this statement? Why or why not?

Chapter Six

The Kingdom of God

WORDS ARE POWERFUL. They're the means of communicating the thoughts of one person to another. Using words, we attempt to draw a picture of the image in our minds so someone else can see what we're thinking.

I'm sure we've all experienced times when we wished we'd chosen different words. The wrong choice of words can inflame a situation or misrepresent our intentions. Jesus was very deliberate in his choice of words when he invited people to enter the kingdom of God.

There are more than a hundred references to the kingdom of God in the New Testament. Jesus began his public ministry with the words, "Repent, for the kingdom of heaven is near" (Matthew 4:17b). Jesus continued for three years to teach about the kingdom through the use of parables that compare everyday life experiences to kingdom life. The question of Jesus being a king and having a kingdom continued to be addressed to the end of his life, even in his trial before Pilate.

LOOKING FOR THE KINGDOM

The concept of the kingdom of God was not new to Israel. The prayer and longing of every devout Jew was for a return to the days when they were politically independent—free from the rule of godless nations like Rome.

Israel had seen its greatest glory under the leadership of kings like David and Solomon. However, with the many kings that followed, the Jews lost touch with the desires of God for their nation. Even though

God sent prophets to try to get them back on course, they refused to change. As a result, the judgment of God came upon them, and they were taken as captives to Babylon. Prophets such as Ezekiel and Daniel promised a time when the kingdom would be reestablished. Ezekiel 21 declared that the crown would be returned to the one to whom it rightfully belonged.

When Jesus spoke of the kingdom of God, his words resonated with the deep longing in the hearts of people who for hundreds of years had been waiting for the promise of the prophets. Luke 23 describes Joseph of Arimathea, who asked for the body of Jesus after the crucifixion, as a good man who was waiting for the kingdom of God.

Yet, the story of the gospels is a story of rejection. With so many waiting for the kingdom, why was Jesus not received? Why did the leadership of Israel want him dead? In John 6:15, Jesus withdrew from a group of people trying to take him by force and make him king. Why? At the beginning of the last week of Jesus's public ministry, the crowds received him into Jerusalem like a king. In less than a week, he was dead. What was the problem?

The Jews wanted a king to throw off the Roman control of their nation. Their desire was not for God and his purposes but rather for independence, military might, and the economic benefits of being a powerful nation.

A Decision

In sharp contrast to the Jews' expectations, Jesus taught in Matthew 5–7 a standard for life in God's kingdom, and in doing so he identified who would be part of this kingdom. Matthew's account gives us the opportunity to listen in and decide for ourselves about the value of what Jesus was offering—and whether we really want to be part of it.

A decision that holds eternal consequences certainly merits a personal investigation of primary sources such as Matthew 5–7. God's provision of the Scriptures gives each of us an opportunity to listen to the Master. In this way, we can compare what others say about him with the record of his words which are preserved for us in the Scriptures.

Qualities of Kingdom Followers

According to Jesus, the kingdom is for those who have a particular need, desire, and willingness.

> Blessed are the poor in spirit, for theirs is the kingdom of heaven. Blessed are those who mourn, for they will be comforted. Blessed are the meek, for they will inherit the earth. Blessed are those who hunger and thirst for righteousness, for they will be filled. Blessed are the merciful, for they will be shown mercy. Blessed are the pure in heart, for they will see God. Blessed are the peacemakers, for they will be called sons of God. Blessed are those who are persecuted because of righteousness, for theirs is the kingdom of heaven. (Matthew 5:3–10)

These verses indicate that the kingdom is for the poor in spirit, those who mourn, the meek, those who hunger and thirst for righteousness, the merciful, the pure in heart, the peacemakers, and those who are persecuted for righteousness.

It isn't hard to see why this description didn't attract people who were looking for power and political freedom. The meek and poor in spirit are not self-sufficient but rather acknowledge their need for God's shepherding. In a similar fashion, those who mourn their losses and their sinful condition and those who hunger and thirst for righteousness want their lives to be as God desires. The peacemakers and the merciful know the heart of God and therefore respond to him by working for peace and being merciful to others. The pure in heart are single-minded in their desire for God and his kingdom. Those who are persecuted for righteousness' sake are willing to give whatever is necessary (even life itself) for the cause of the kingdom.

It's important to note that simply "not wanting to go to hell" did not make the list of requirements! The few who travel the narrow road do so in pursuit of God rather than for selfish reasons.

STANDARDS FOR THE KINGDOM

In the section of this sermon starting at Matthew 5:21, Jesus takes the laws of Israel to a whole new level. He deepens these outward rules such as "do not kill" and "do not commit adultery" and calls for his followers to not be angry or lust. Jesus transformed outward laws into inward attitudes that Jeremiah said God would write on the hearts of his people (Jeremiah 31:31). Everything from taking vows and retaliation to love itself is given a totally different perspective through life in God's kingdom.

In Matthew 6, Jesus focuses on the revered marks of Jewish piety: alms, prayer, and fasting. He moves these actions out of the public eye to the secret place before God. Jesus ends this chapter by addressing the issue of money and how the pursuit of the kingdom comes first.

Matthew 7 mentions the small gate and narrow road while giving a warning about false teachers and false professions of faith. Jesus ends this teaching with the statement that only those who do the will of the Father will enter the kingdom of heaven. His final parable concerning house building makes the point that those who hear but refuse to do God's Word are like the one who builds his house on sand. In the end, his house will not stand.

GOD ENABLES WHAT HE DESIRES

God expects us to do his will in order to participate in his kingdom. But there is a problem here: the goal is unreachable if attempted alone. Paul adamantly challenges any thought that one can be justified before God through his or her ability to keep God's laws. "We who are Jews by birth and not Gentile sinners know that a man is not justified by observing the law, but by faith in Jesus Christ. So we, too, have put our faith in Christ Jesus that we may be justified by faith in Christ and not by observing the law, because by observing the law no one will be justified" (Galatians 2:15–16).

However, God's supernatural provision of rebirth and his indwelling Spirit make possible the impossible. God enables what he desires for those willing to enter his kingdom and be empowered by his Spirit. Paul explains this principle: "For what the law was powerless to do in that it

was weakened by the sinful nature, God did by sending his own Son in the likeness of sinful man to be a sin offering. And so he condemned sin in sinful man, in order that the righteous requirements of the law might be fully met in us, who do not live according to the sinful nature but according to the Spirit" (Romans 8:3–4).

Jesus says, "Do not be afraid, little flock, for your Father has been pleased to give you the kingdom" (Luke 12:32). God's desire to give us the kingdom is an important part of the good news that Jesus announced. God takes the initiative in approaching us so we can make a response of faith. God has given the means through Jesus's death, which allows entry into his kingdom. The gift of spiritual rebirth and God's indwelling presence provide the transformation needed for life according to the standard of the kingdom. However, the gift of the kingdom does not negate the demand of the kingdom.

Balancing the gift and demand of the kingdom is a delicate challenge. The opportunity to enter the kingdom is absolutely based on the gift of God. However, God's kingdom is still just that: his kingdom, his will, his standard, and his way of life—not ours.

Few Saved?

Among the Jews, the party of the Sadducees did not believe in the resurrection, and they made the challenge to Jesus that the idea of the resurrection presents too many unsolvable problems. On the other hand, the party of the Pharisees embraced the concept of the future kingdom when they would sit at table with Abraham, Isaac, and Jacob. The Jews often debated who would be saved and whether there would be few or many. One theory was that all Jews would be saved simply on the basis of being sons of Abraham, except for a few Jews who were harsh criminals or heretics. Others believed that only those belonging to a particular sect within Judaism would be saved. This question was presented to Jesus.

> Someone asked him, "Lord, are only a few people going to be saved?" He said to them, "Make every effort to enter through the

narrow door, because many, I tell you, will try to enter and will not be able to." (Luke 13:23–24)

The original text uses the Greek word *agonia*, which is translated as "make every effort" to enter. Connecting *agonia* to the English *agonize* helps emphasize the power of the word being used. We must "agonize to enter"—a wholehearted effort is required to enter the kingdom. One can be bothered or concerned about something, but to agonize over it takes the situation to an entirely different level! Obviously, one does not enter the kingdom of God by slipping on a rock and falling into the water. An all-out effort and consuming passion accompany those who are a part of God's kingdom. Maybe that's why Jesus said only a few will find the small gate to life.

Taking Appropriate Action

The intensity of Jesus's words and the level of commitment he expects are just too much for some people. Therefore, I encourage you to keep reminding yourself of the depth of what accompanies Jesus's offer of the kingdom. His standards are life-giving principles. Yielding to God as king is the only appropriate response to the God of the universe. Connection with God establishes an eternal relationship full of intended purposes yet to be fulfilled. Being spiritually transformed and having God as our Father gives us a new way of life. In the words of Jesus, God's kingdom is a treasure worth selling all to have.

Jesus gives a parable in Matthew 22 concerning a king who gave a wedding feast for his son. Those initially invited made light of the invitation and went their own way. As a result, the king sent his servants into the streets to invite as many as they could find, stating that those initially invited didn't deserve to come.

When the king came in to meet the guests, he found one without a wedding garment and had him removed from the celebration. It's not clear whether the man failed to put on the wedding garment provided by the king or if he didn't reverence the king's invitation enough to go home first and change. It is clear that his lack of appropriate action insulted the king.

Everyone must be attentive to the warning that the gate is small, the way is narrow, and only a few are willing to submit to God's standard. Jesus's call to make every effort to enter the gate points to distractions and outright obstacles that stand in the way of our appropriate response of faith. You must ask the question of whether you have the level of passion required for God's kingdom. Only you know whether your heart is yielded to the One who made you and calls you to his purpose for your life.

My Kingdom or God's?

The Jews wanted a political kingdom, a visible display of military might, and the tangible enjoyment of prosperity. This sounds a lot like the distortions of Christianity being preached today!

Jesus established God's kingdom in a fashion that accomplishes God's intentions rather than the Jews' desires. In keeping with this, each of us must examine closely the driving force that motivates our interest in God's kingdom. "What's in it for me" dominates too much of what the modern world pursues in life. Unless our focus is on God and his purpose, we'll make the mistake of attempting to get God's blessing on our kingdom rather than joining his. Some think they can give God lip service enough to cash in at death but otherwise go about building their own kingdoms in this life. However, Jesus says, "Seek first his kingdom and his righteousness" (Matthew 6:33a).

The broad way of life is selfish and me-centered. The way of the kingdom is loving and God-centered. "My kingdom or God's kingdom" is a choice we all must make. It's the call to live the life of self-giving love that originates from our heavenly Father. We must make every effort not to pass up the joy and fulfillment of God's purpose for our lives. Even with all of this available and so much at stake, many go the opposite direction when approached by God.

The Opposite Direction

Recently something happened on the farm that reminded me of the response many make when God approaches them about entering his kingdom. On this particular day, my border collie, Sada, had been alerting me to the fact that a new calf was bedded down in the woods next to our house. I finally went with her to check on it. When I examined the calf, she responded in fear and went running down the hill. At the bottom, she turned and fled to the back part of the farm. I followed to return her to the field where she could reconnect with her mother. Much to my amazement, when I entered that field, the calf ran through the back fence, plunged into the creek, and began going downstream. Once in the stream, I knew she wouldn't be able to find her way back home.

The poor calf was in quite a dilemma—running from one who had only good intentions for her. The path she took downstream was leading to her death, but my approach to her was outside of any comfortable experience in her short life, and she reacted in fear.

Sada and I ran through the woods to get ahead of the calf and turn her back upstream. She'd made it quite a way before we passed her. It was early spring, and a spring-fed creek is very cold, requiring a hearty commitment to enter!

Even with both the dog and me in front of her, the calf kept coming downstream rather than turning around. I tackled her and held on while getting my belt off to use as a lead rope to take her home. My attempt to lead her back to the farm was met with bold resistance. Slipping and falling in the creek while dragging a stiff-necked calf was quite the task! She ignored my attempt to tell her she was going in the wrong direction. My warning that she was choosing death by fighting against me was rejected as well.

Finally we were out of the stream and on our way back to the calf's mother. The three of us crossing the field made a thought-provoking picture. On my left was Sada, a dog who would follow me off a cliff, and on my right was a calf resisting my every effort to give her life. Unlike the calf, my border collie loves and trusts me. I don't need a lead rope for her. In fact, I can't get out of her sight even when I want to. On the other extreme was the calf, who didn't have any understanding of my intentions for her life.

Sada and I got mom and calf reunited and made our way home back

up the hill. Sada was thrilled to have been on another adventure with me, and I'd heard God speak to me through an everyday experience of life. He's fond of using these kinds of events to teach us about the kingdom.

DON'T RESIST

Have you ever run in the opposite direction from the Good Shepherd? He doesn't give up or quit when we go the wrong way. His pursuit of us is driven by his desire to give us life. God wants us to be like Sada: loving and trusting him and feeling thrilled to be with him doing whatever needs to be done. God's ways are like the lead rope I used with the calf. They keep us from going in the direction that leads to death. The less we resist them by trusting the Shepherd, the easier it is to enjoy the life he's trying to give.

Sada is teaching me how I should behave in the kingdom. It's about walking with God without a lead rope, wanting to be there, and not letting the Shepherd get out of my sight. If Sada could talk, she'd say, "I'd rather be on an adventure with my master than eat when I'm hungry." For her, there are no words more exciting to hear than, "Come, we have things to do." She doesn't ask why, when we'll be back, if she'll miss supper, or if it's going to be hard. At the sound of my voice, her ears stand up, her eyes sparkle, and every fiber of her being responds in joy to the pleasure of hearing my call.

Sada doesn't mind being under my authority. In fact, she thrives on it. She wants to please me and would risk her life to do whatever she thinks I want. I can only hope that my desire for and need for God's leadership in my life will one day match Sada's dedication to me. Not all dogs are geared like Sada, just as not all people are willing to respond to God's prompting concerning his kingdom. It's your choice to lay on the couch with the remote, or to always be looking, listening, and waiting for the Master's call to go on a kingdom adventure.

SEEING WHAT OTHERS PASS BY

God's kingdom means a different way to live. God's kingdom is a special realm in which life is experienced in fullness by following the will of the

Father. Those who see what others pass by make an all-out effort, letting nothing stand in their way so they can experience the joy of life with God in his kingdom.

When all is said and done, *kingdom* is the right word to describe the setting for our relationship with God. God is king, and he does rule. However, unlike expressions of kingdom in our world, our king dies so that we can live, and rules so that we can find life. Don't let anything distract you or stand in your way as you diligently and continuously pursue the One who touches your life, inviting you to enter the small gate of his kingdom leading to the fullness of life.

REFLECTING ON CHAPTER 6

The Jews wanted a powerful political kingdom with accompanying economic benefits. Jesus offered instead a spiritual kingdom that has eternal purposes. In what ways have you been similarly misguided as to what Jesus is offering? In what ways are many expressions of modern Christianity off track with what Jesus taught concerning what it means to be in the kingdom?

How does one balance accepting the gift of the kingdom with the expected response to the demands of the King?

Many go in the opposite direction when offered the life-giving ways of God's kingdom. How can his followers reflect the life-giving quality of the kingdom to others?

Chapter Seven

A Way of Life

WHEN PEOPLE FIND OUT I raise cattle, they often say, "I always thought it would be nice to live on a farm." My response is that we need to have this conversation during what I call "I love farming" weather! Late January, with a blue-blowing snow and temperatures in the single digits, might be the right time to assess your compatibility with farm living. Another good time to see how "nice" it would be to have a farm is early spring, when a storm puts a tree across a fence and you have to make repairs with the wind and rain coming at you sideways.

My point to these folks is that farming is every day, regardless of the weather or our preference to sit in comfortable dry clothes by a warm fire. I live on a farm because it's the way of life I prefer. And for those of us who love the land, this daily commitment, regardless of the weather, is not a chore.

Farming is not only a daily commitment, it's also a different way of life. I love the farm, first and foremost because farming is done outside. I enjoy working with my hands and exerting myself physically. Riding the tractor gives me stress therapy that no counselor or pill could ever provide. The different seasons, the miracle of life in plants and animals, and being in touch with the life-giving power of the land make me constantly aware of my Creator.

WAY OF LIFE

In a similar fashion, life in the kingdom is a daily commitment to a different

way of life. Having an emotional moment is not real Christianity. Neither does going to church, listening to the sermon, and enjoying the accompanying musical concert comprise what it means to live in God's kingdom. The essence of what it means to be a Christian and to live the kingdom way of life is found in how we work, live at home, interact with others, and follow Jesus as our shepherd.

Sadly, many people involved in church are not even familiar with the kingdom way of life. When it comes to their day-to-day activity, there's little difference in how they live as compared to those outside of the church—for example, problem marriages and divorce are just as prevalent inside the church as outside. Most professing Christians blend into our cultural way of life with little distinction.

GOD'S UNIQUE KINGDOM

God has structured his kingdom in a way that enables everyone to participate fully in what he is doing. Living in the kingdom is not just for those in paid positions of ministry, people who go to Africa, or those who enroll in the seminary.

At the time of his crucifixion, Jesus explained to Pilate the uniqueness of his kingdom. "My kingdom is not of this world. If it were, my servants would fight to prevent my arrest by the Jews. But now my kingdom is from another place" (John 18:36). The idea of a kingdom not of this world and from another place presents many intriguing questions. The fact that his servants did not fight for his release reveals that Jesus's kingdom works quite differently than the kingdoms of the world.

WHATEVER YOU DO

One example of life in God's unique kingdom is given by the apostle Paul in his letter to the Colossian church. The call of the kingdom is not to retreat to a monastery or achieve some great spiritual quest. First and foremost, the call of the kingdom is allowing God to be part of the moment-by-moment living of our lives. Paul describes how this works: "And whatever you do, whether in word or deed, do it all in the name

of the Lord Jesus, giving thanks to God the Father through him" (Colossians 3:17).

This verse challenges our tendency to separate things into sacred and secular. "Whatever you do" makes *all* of life sacred. There's never a time when what we're doing is outside of the kingdom. When all our words and deeds are done in the name of the Lord Jesus, they will be consistent with his character. By living this way, we represent Jesus to our world and demonstrate our conviction that Jesus is the model for how life should be lived.

As Serving the Lord

To strengthen what he was saying, Paul added the following instruction: "Whatever you do, work at it with all your heart, as working for the Lord, not for men, since you know that you will receive an inheritance from the Lord as a reward. It is the Lord Christ you are serving" (Colossians 3:23–24). This statement concerning work was spoken to slaves. They didn't have a choice about what, when, or how much they were required to do. Usually, unpleasant and demeaning tasks were reserved for them. Yet, Paul challenged this group to do their work as serving the Lord.

Viewing every task as one in which we are serving the Lord should create an enormous change in the way we approach life. Our willingness to face thankless tasks in honor of Christ demonstrates our love for him. However, the ability to live by this different viewpoint of life requires discipline and desire which are motivated by love.

The principle of serving Jesus through serving others originates in his teachings. In Matthew 25:35–46, when talking about the final judgment, Jesus said that all acts of mercy in meeting the needs of others would be counted as if they were completed for him. Our acts of mercy are to be extended to the deserving and undeserving alike even in the face of injustice. Remember, mercy is not based in justice, but rather in grace. Peter, speaking of Jesus, writes, "When they hurled their insults at him, he did not retaliate; when he suffered, he made no threats. Instead, he entrusted himself to him who judges justly" (1 Peter 2:23).

When "whatever we do in word or deed" is focused upon Jesus, as

if serving him, life is radically changed. Can you imagine what life would be like if all Christians followed this kingdom ethic? Try to picture living among a group of people whose words and deeds were always expressed within the character of Jesus. What would marriage be like if every spouse spoke as Jesus spoke and took action with the compassion and sensitivity of our Lord? Employers and employees could revolutionize the workplace if this standard of kingdom life was lived out!

NOT PRACTICAL OR BINDING

However, many regard this part of the kingdom ethic as not practical or binding in a modern world. Some would even say, "Who would want to do that?" Not long ago, it became fashionable to wear a WWJD ("What Would Jesus Do?") bracelet. It is easy to wear a bracelet, but more than jewelry is needed to empower this kingdom way of life. How much we admire and love Jesus and how much we want to say "thank you" for the mercy we have received makes the difference in how fully we embrace this life-giving and life-changing way of the kingdom.

If you accept the "whatever you do" principle of kingdom life, the real test of your personal expression of Christianity will be best attested to by those you live and work with. Do those who know you best admire who you are as a Christian? Do those within your community who desperately depend on help from others know who you are by your acts of mercy? The little things, such as how respectfully we treat the waitress serving us our meal and whether or not we leave a generous tip, speak a great deal about our Christianity.

Regulating our lives by the "whatever you do in word or deed" principle is not only appropriate but radically needed in a world in crisis. Spouses, children, and others need to be touched by this kingdom ethic so that they will want to live by this standard as well.

The true test of our commitment is when we're called upon to represent Jesus in a task that is unpleasant, unfair, or mundane. When circumstances are unfair and we still yield ourselves to words and deeds that exemplify Christ, we allow God to shape us into his likeness and strengthen our love relationship with him. In this way, all of life is an act

of worship. Whether we're making a living, cleaning up our family's messes, or teaching a Sunday school class, each life situation is an expression of our relationship with God.

It is exciting that we have the opportunity to work for and participate with our Lord in whatever we're doing. This unique feature of the kingdom is truly awesome. Life in God's kingdom is not made up of occasional moments or done on a part-time basis. It is a unique way of living that touches all we say and do.

Though I live on a farm, I make my living as pastor and only farm on occasion. As a result, I mend a lot of my fences with the aid of a flashlight, and my management of the land and animals is completed irregularly, whenever I can get to it. A visit to my farm would quickly show that I'm not raising cattle full-time. In the same way, others (especially those who know us best) should be able to observe by our lives whether we are living in the kingdom on a part-time or full-time basis.

JESUS MAKING HIMSELF KNOWN

Jesus adds an additional piece to what we have been discussing: "Whoever has my commands and obeys them, he is the one who loves me. He who loves me will be loved by my Father, and I too will love him and show myself to him" (John 14:21). Jesus promises to make himself real to all who obey him. When we demonstrate our love for him in word and deed, Jesus reveals himself to us in these moments, inspiring and empowering the task. Inviting Jesus to participate with us as we obey him and serve him in *all* we do takes all of life to a sacred level. We are changed, the world is touched, and Jesus is glorified.

My father taught me to see my work as a presentation of myself. My character, work ethic, and integrity were on display in everything that I did. If Jesus is the one I want to please, be like, and serve, then my words, actions, and attitudes will display it.

The point is this: If you love Jesus, you will want to please him and honor him. If you do everything as if you're serving him, you will be continually aware of his presence as opposed to simply having moments of spiritual activity. Every task and conversation takes on a whole new

meaning when addressed in this way. How you speak to your wife or husband, how you do your tasks at home or on the job, how you interact with your children and others, and how you involve yourself in church become monitors of whether the kingdom is truly where you live.

Those who've experienced forgiveness and the change that new birth brings don't have to long for the opportunity to thank the One who has given them life. When we serve God by actively living each day in a sacred partnership with him, no matter what we are doing, we push back the darkness of our world enough to allow others to catch a glimpse of Jesus.

Have-To Responsibility or Opportunity?

Just as farming is not for everyone, the way of life of the kingdom does not appeal to everyone. To farm, you must love the land, the outdoors, and the daily contact with the ongoing cycles of life. Equally so, for the kingdom way of life to be appealing, you must love God, want to be in touch with him constantly, and thrive on his life-giving ways. This daily call of the kingdom can be viewed as a have-to responsibility, or you can see it as the opportunity of a lifetime.

When people tell me they think it would be nice to live on a farm, I tell them to think long and hard as to whether they're suited for the farming way of life. Farming is every day, it's different, the work's never done, and physical activity is required in all kinds of weather, so be sure of what you're getting into.

The kingdom is a different way of life as well. Because we love and admire Jesus and agree with his life-giving ways, we will endeavor to be like him and serve him in everything we do. His goal of making the kingdom visible to a world of darkness is now our goal as well.

Is the challenge of living the kingdom way of life a "do I have to" task for you? Is it a cross to bear? Or have you seen enough to know that the kingdom is life?

Personal Inventory

It can be helpful to take a personal inventory when discussing concepts like this. In what ways do you violate the standard of life Jesus lived? Are

you personally committed to the kingdom's life-giving ways? Do you have a desire to honor the King of the kingdom? Or do you find other things more appealing?

Maybe we need to get a little more specific in how we apply this kingdom concept. Did Jesus argue? Was he rude, self-seeking? Did he respond to the needs of others? Carry others' burdens? Did he react to every unfair or unkind statement addressed to him? Was he always sensitive and willing to help those in pain? Do you know Jesus well enough to have a clear picture of how he dealt with life so that you can allow his life to affect yours?

When it comes to farming, hay must be put up at the hottest time of the year and taken out again to feed when it's coldest. There are chores to do like mending fences, repairing the barn, and attending to the needs of the cattle. But these activities are not have-to chores: rather, they are *why* one chooses life on a farm! The way of life of the kingdom is to be in God's presence continually. We do what we do as serving him and in his character, and by doing so we join him in making his kingdom visible to our world. This is not a have-to—it is why we joined his kingdom.

My wife's grandmother told us, "Don't buy a farm, because the work is never done!" But she missed the point. We bought the farm because it is how we chose to live. Personally, I don't find pleasure sitting in the recliner with a TV remote in my hand. I want to be outside working with the animals, mending fences, and crossing the creek when necessary to return the strays. I don't *want* the work to be done. There's nothing like being outside in the rain, cold, and heat; there's nothing like the beauty of spring or the glory of fall or the wonder of a fresh-fallen snow. Farm living is truly different, and it's not for everyone. Equally so, the way of life of the kingdom is not for everyone. It's only for those who see what others pass by.

Living in a Distinct Way

In the Old Testament, the Jews stood out as unique among the nations around them. They spoke Hebrew, circumcised their male children, had particular rules about what they ate, rested on the Sabbath, served only

one God, and didn't use idols in their worship. However, these outward expressions of their religion were far from God's ultimate plan for them.

Moses expressed the definitive mark of what it means to be God's people when he prayed, "If your Presence does not go with us, do not send us up from here. How will anyone know that you are pleased with me and with your people unless you go with us? What else will distinguish me and your people from all the other people on the face of the earth?" (Exodus 33:15–16).

It would be easy to assume that we're living differently just because we go to church. But our true uniqueness as Christians is evident when God goes with us, and when everything we do is done in his character and as serving him. Christians who have been truly transformed by God stand out. They are those who love their wives as Christ loved the church, who walk in love as Christ loved us, and who bring the light of the kingdom into a world of darkness.

The Model

Paul does a good job in Romans 12:9–18 of describing what the kingdom way of life looks like:

> Love must be sincere. Hate what is evil; cling to what is good. Be devoted to one another in brotherly love. Honor one another above yourselves. Never be lacking in zeal, but keep your spiritual fervor, serving the Lord. Be joyful in hope, patient in affliction, faithful in prayer. Share with God's people who are in need. Practice hospitality. Bless those who persecute you; bless and do not curse. Rejoice with those who rejoice; mourn with those who mourn. Live in harmony with one another. Do not be proud, but be willing to associate with people of low position. Do not be conceited. Do not repay anyone evil for evil. Be careful to do what is right in the eyes of everybody. If it is possible, as far as it depends on you, live at peace with everyone.

To follow Paul's words is to live the way of life of the kingdom. It is

different. It is what shapes us, gives us life, and allows others to see the beauty of God's kingdom.

REFLECTING ON CHAPTER 7

Do you desire this type of life in God's kingdom? If so, in what areas of your life do you make a conscious effort to live this way? In what relationships or situations do you most struggle to be Christlike?

Can a true believer have no desire for kingdom life?

Being in the kingdom of God involves our total way of life. However, many think the demands of Christianity are fulfilled by going to church on Sunday. What do you feel has led to this major separation between what Jesus taught and what people have come to believe is the essence of Christianity?

Chapter Eight

Weeds Don't Need Any Help

As you travel the narrow road of God's kingdom, you'll find the path to be rather restricted. You won't travel with a crowd, yet you won't travel alone. God goes with you. The narrowness of the road has its benefits, because the journey's difficulties make it clear that you need God's indwelling to stay on course. Requiring God's help isn't a sign of weakness, but rather a purposefully designed feature of the road you travel.

Jesus used the following parable to describe one piece of the struggle of life in the kingdom:

> Listen! A farmer went out to sow his seed. As he was scattering the seed, some fell along the path, and the birds came and ate it up. Some fell on rocky places, where it did not have much soil. It sprang up quickly, because the soil was shallow. But when the sun came up, the plants were scorched, and they withered because they had no root. Other seed fell among thorns, which grew up and choked the plants, so that they did not bear grain. Still other seed fell on good soil. It came up, grew and produced a crop multiplying thirty, sixty, or even a hundred times. (Mark 4:3–8)

At the mere mention of thorns and weeds, farmers want to spit, stomp their feet, and say words not fit for Sunday school. Weeds are a constant battle and a threat to every farmer's way of life.

With the industrialization of America, our modern generation has lost contact with the land. Therefore, Jesus's use of weeds as a metaphor for his thoughts has lost some of its power—but it's extremely effective when it's really understood. A recent experience I had on the farm might help some of you understand the magnitude of Jesus's words about thorns and weeds in the kingdom of God.

Visiting My Old Friend

I had the opportunity a few years ago to rent a farm close to mine. A couple of the back fields had been lying fallow for a while. As a result of this neglect, the fields were a mess. For three years, I managed those fields by mowing appropriately and adding nutrients to the soil through the application of fertilizer. The fruit of my labor was a nice stand of grass that yielded a much-valued hay crop. As my daddy often said, "The grass in this field is as thick as the hair on a dog's back."

The owner decided to rent to another farmer, so for three years someone else had control of those fields. The new renter contacted me about harvesting some hay on a portion of the land, and as a gesture of appreciation, I volunteered to do some mowing around the farm.

Having worked that farm for three years, I felt like I was visiting an old friend. Harvesting hay requires many trips through a field, bringing familiarity with every little bump, hole, and change of elevation. The back fields ran along a spring-fed creek, and during the fall the fence rows were lined with trees changing colors. I was eager to see the land that had worked with me to produce several good hay crops.

As I crossed the big drainage ditch and rode up in full view of the field, I was overwhelmed. Weeds and thorns had covered it—with no grass in sight! I didn't expect to see the land struggling under the weight of this invasion of weeds. It hadn't been that long ago when the field was producing a nice crop of hay.

Weeds of all shapes and varieties were eliminating any chance for the grass to thrive. Everything from goldenrod to the worst varmint of all weeds, thistles, was towering where there was once a beautiful hay field.

Like a military tank armed for battle, my tractor pushed relentlessly through the field. Weeds stood high enough to block my view, and hordes of insects pounded me in the face as I started mowing. After a couple of laps around the field, pollen and grass seed covered me and the tractor like a yellow blanket. Eventually, as the land began to clear, I could see a stand of grass that had been desperately fighting to stay alive. At the end of the day, the field was clean.

As I sat on my tractor looking across the newly mown field, I knew the battle had only begun. It would take fertilizer and the addition of clover grasses to give the extra punch needed for the grass to fully recover. Weed seeds had been scattered, and more weeds would come back from the root system. Some people, considering the magnitude of the problem, would have filled a sprayer and given the weeds what they deserved. However, since I am a Vietnam veteran aware of the aftereffects of Agent Orange, I try to manage my fields in other ways than blasting them with chemicals.

Uninvited Destruction

Weeds flourish without any assistance and do not need an invitation to show up in a field. All they need is for someone to neglect the grass. Weeds also grow at the speed of light. That is why old folks used to say the kids were "growing like weeds." In a matter of days, weeds can rise above the grass and shade out the sunlight. Unmanaged weeds take the lion's share of any available nutrients and moisture. Soon, the grass has no chance.

Jesus explained the competing power of weeds when he said, "Still others, like seed sown among thorns, hear the word; but the worries of this life, the deceitfulness of wealth and the desires for other things come in and choke the word, making it unfruitful" (Mark 4:18–19). The call of the kingdom needs to be protected, or weeds will choke out the stirring of God within us. If we allow weeds to take over, the only thing in life that matters—our opportunity to be in God's kingdom—will be destroyed.

Taking Action

The battle with weeds in the kingdom of God is a familiar one for seasoned Christians. Like the field I mowed, there's the constant need to clean up our lives by confession and repentance. Confession is to admit guilt and agree with God that an action was wrong. Repentance is to be sorry for what was done and commit to change. God's forgiveness cleanses the field of the weeds.

Clearing the field is the proper first step, but seeds and root systems are in place that will bring new weeds. There's a lot to learn before the battle with weeds is brought under control.

With the purchase of our farm, we inherited a crop of thistles, ironweed, buttercup, and cockleburs scattered throughout the fields. Every time a cocklebur picked up its head, I would cut it off. Mowing cockleburs before they turn to seed is an effective control measure because it breaks their seed cycle. However, since thistles come back from their root systems, my wife, Gale, continually walks our farm with a shovel in her hand on a crusade to take out by the roots every thistle with the audacity to want to spread its seed. Buttercups are about to make me break my no-chemical ban, because I'm not sure I'll ever be free of them otherwise.

In terms of the kingdom, repentance, confession, and forgiveness are the place to start, but the weeds are going to come back. We must stay alert to cut off any competing desire before it has a chance to grow. Some issues are deeply rooted and require a shovel if they're to be eliminated.

For example, Jesus said that the battle with adultery must be cut off with the first appearance of lust. Even deeper than lust is the question of whether we think that we're being deprived of something good outside of the commands of God. In Genesis 3 the serpent tried successfully to convince Eve that God was keeping something good from her that eating the forbidden fruit would provide. Questioning God's character in this way continues to be an obstacle for some people.

Competing desires seek to unseat God as first in our lives. The weeds of worry and the deceitfulness of wealth challenge our trust in God. The

mistaken desire to find life in other ways other than in the kingdom questions God's desire to give us life.

Some weeds are controlled by breaking the seed cycle, while others have to come out by the roots. Still other weeds flourish because of a failure to take care of the soil.

SOUR GROUND

In our part of the country, sage grass turns a golden brown in the fall. It stands up tall and looks quite pretty, but cows don't eat it. When old farmers see a stand of sage grass, they say, "You've got some sour ground there." The more technical explanation is that the pH is out of balance. When the soil is too acidic, sage grass takes over. The solution is to make the soil more alkaline with the application of lime (calcium carbonate). When the soil is balanced properly, good grasses can grow.

John the Baptist told his disciples that he had to decrease while Jesus increased. The concept of Jesus being in us works a lot like balancing the pH of the soil. When the "I" in my life is out of balance with the control Jesus should have, then the soil of my life gets sour, and weeds have a great opportunity to thrive. However, when Jesus is allowed to increase, the pH is balanced properly and the good grasses of the kingdom have opportunity to grow.

EARLY DETECTION

Weeds stand out clearly when one is interested in producing grass. When I walk my fields, I'm keenly aware of the level of clover grasses that produce nitrogen to promote grass production. I constantly monitor the level of good grasses that will produce the rich protein my cows need. Weeds are like neon signs to a conscientious farmer.

Paul said, "We demolish arguments and every pretension that sets itself up against the knowledge of God, and we take captive every thought to make it obedient to Christ" (2 Corinthians 10:5). The discipline of addressing our thoughts to make them obedient to Christ can have revolutionary results. If you approach the kingdom this way, weeds will be removed before they can gain a death grip on your spiritual walk.

In Galatians 5, Paul provides a list identifying the fruit of the Spirit as opposed to the fruit of the selfish nature:

> The acts of the sinful nature are obvious: sexual immorality, impurity and debauchery; idolatry and witchcraft; hatred, discord, jealousy, fits of rage, selfish ambition, dissensions, factions and envy; drunkenness, orgies, and the like. I warn you, as I did before, that those who live like this will not inherit the kingdom of God. But the fruit of the Spirit is love, joy, peace, patience, kindness, goodness, faithfulness, gentleness and self-control . . . Since we live by the Spirit, let us keep in step with the Spirit. (Galatians 5:19–23, 25)

It is easy to focus on the part of the list mentioning orgies, witchcraft, and drunkenness and be confident that we don't do those things. However, the list also speaks of hatred, discord, envy, dissensions, and selfish ambition, which are not as easy to dodge.

Equally so, the fruit of the Spirit is not idealistic poetry but rather what happens when Jesus is allowed to increase in us as we decrease. Life radically changes when all that we do is accompanied by love, joy, peace, patience, kindness, goodness, faithfulness, gentleness, and self-control. But what's possible through the Spirit is cut off if we do not decisively deal with the competing desires of weeds.

The fruit of our lives can be very telling. For example, what do you get when you squeeze an orange? Obviously, you get orange juice—what's on the inside. When life squeezes us, what do you get? Hopefully, we give evidence of God's Spirit dwelling within us.

All desires that compete with the kingdom find their source in our selfish natures. James makes it clear what the source of temptation is when he says, "But each one is tempted when, by his own evil desire, he is dragged away and enticed" (James 1:14). The contrast between our selfish natures and godly character should make it easy to recognize a weed when we see one.

As followers of the kingdom, we must be aware of the seed-sowing

machines all around us. Movies, magazines, conversations, lifestyles, and marketing gimmicks constantly bombard us with suggestions that compete with kingdom life. Slick, inviting advertisements continuously seek to persuade us that we must have whatever someone is trying to sell in order to be happy.

If we let these seeds grow, the weeds produced will choke out our desire for the kingdom way of life. If we let our lives get too acidic by focusing on "I" instead of Jesus, these competing suggestions will flourish. All that the world pitches at us appeals to our strong, innate selfishness. The promise of pleasure and self-satisfaction is hard to refuse. However, God is calling us to a level of life much higher than selfish gratification.

DOING NOTHING

Grass needs help to grow. Weeds simply need for you to do nothing. When you see a field, check to see if the farmer is managing it properly. A field of blue-green grass flowing in the wind doesn't just happen. Someone did something on purpose.

When the land manager is doing nothing, weeds show up and destroy every good intention for a harvest. Weeds bring death. They're great at blocking out the light. Jesus intended for his audience to hear the gravity of his parable, lest they be victims of the power of weeds.

THE GOOD STUFF

There's a big difference in food value and protein levels from one type of grass to another. The better grasses, like timothy, orchard grass, and alfalfa are high in protein but require reseeding to keep them going. We say in the country that the good stuff "plays out," so it must constantly be reseeded. The seed of the kingdom is the Word of God. To make the good grass flourish, we must constantly reseed the soil of our lives with study and meditation on the Word.

In my area, we depend on fescue grass because of its hardiness and ability to survive and keep coming back. One can get by with fescue, but the better grasses produce a better calf crop. Many Christians are not

reseeding through personal study of God's Word and therefore are just surviving spiritually. It requires extra effort to have a rich crop of the "good stuff."

Joining a Bible study group; doing some reading in the arenas of church history, apologetics, or philosophy; and reading commentaries and systematic theologies will deepen your appreciation and involvement in our faith. We have a rich heritage of great thinkers and godly people who offer thought-provoking inquiry into the deeper nuances of the faith. To love God with all of your mind is to explore questions and gain a background understanding of the tenets of our faith that many just memorize without appreciation for the questions they seek to answer.

When caring for soil, there's more to do than just balance the pH. Nutrients such as potash, nitrogen, and other substances are added to the soil to feed the grass. When compost is prepared for use as a fertilizer, leaves and other organic materials are allowed to die and decay to provide food for the grass or other crops. Like compost, dying to self is part of the call of the kingdom. The death of self becomes like compost that feeds life in the kingdom and allows us to experience a harvest that is thirty, sixty, or a hundredfold.

DAILY REMINDERS

When Jesus spoke in parables, he used simple stories taken from real life to communicate the truths of the kingdom. Since the parables used everyday images, his audience could be reminded daily of the eternal truths that the parables conveyed.

Every stand of grass or lawn you see can trigger thoughts about your own spiritual battle with weeds. Each field and lawn speaks volumes about its caretaker. If you know a spiritual weed when you see one, you have an advantage. You can cut the weed down to interrupt the seed cycle or dig it out by the roots and then feed the soil. As a result, you'll enjoy greater benefits of life in the kingdom. Those who carefully balance their pH and constantly reseed will allow the word of the kingdom to produce the intended harvest in their lives.

Though I raise cattle, in reality I'm a grass producer. If there's no

grass, then there won't be any cattle. Taking it a step further, I'm a weed fighter. If there is ever going to be any grass for the cows to eat, I must deal with weeds.

To say I'm a kingdom follower is to say I fight weeds. The level to which I tend the soil of my life, seed and reseed, and cut down and dig up by the roots every competing desire is the level to which I enjoy life in the kingdom.

Our lives are vivid expressions of whether we've tended the soil, reseeded, and fought the battle with weeds. Remember, doing nothing spiritually allows weeds to choke out the kingdom grasses. However, by taking purposeful action, you can help ensure that the good, nutrient-rich grass of the kingdom will grow in your life and provide the life-giving harvest God intended.

REFLECTING ON CHAPTER 8

The weeds of competing desires seek to block out the light and absorb the nutrients that make the grass of the kingdom grow. In what ways can you prioritize your time and energy in order to grow your relationship with God?

What are some weed-sowing machines that all of us must struggle with in life (TV shows, certain movies, particular leisure activities, etc.)?

Is the soil of your life acidic? Does the "I" overpower the control Jesus should have? What signals in your life tell you that you are out of balance?

In what ways do you reseed so the good grass of the kingdom can thrive?

Chapter Nine

God Is the Viticulturist

WHAT IN THE WORLD IS A VITICULTURIST? Is it like *anthropomorphic* or one of those other Greek-based philosophical words we use to talk about God? Actually, the term comes from the world of horticulture. Once I tell you that *viti* is the Latin root for *vine,* you can probably derive the meaning of *viticulturist.*

In John 15, Jesus says he is the vine, we are the branches, and his Father is the gardener—the viticulturist, the vinedresser. This parable illustrates an important aspect of the spiritual relationship we share with God in his kingdom.

THE MASTER VINEDRESSER

In Jesus's day, people had great respect for the vinedresser. They knew firsthand the difference in the quality of the grapes under the care of a master vinedresser. Allowing God to be involved in our lives as a viticulturist can make a vast difference in the quality of our lives in his kingdom.

Grapes are one of the oldest cultivated fruits. The use of grapes goes back as far as the earliest recorded civilization. For thousands of years, people have been tending grape vines. Today, there are college degree programs in viticulture (the cultivation of grapes) and enology (the science of wine making). With an entire college curriculum based on raising and processing grapes, there's obviously a lot to know about being a viticulturist!

The production of quality grapes requires intricate and careful management. High-quality grapes can be made into wine that commands thousands of dollars per bottle. On the other hand, grapes only good enough for jelly yield significantly lower prices.

Through Us

The parable of the vine reveals a deep truth about the kingdom of God. The spiritual concepts of being born from above and the Father making his home in us describe something supernatural that happens *to* us. With the vine parable, Jesus is saying that something not only happens to us, but something also happens *through* us.

The natural process of sap moving from the vine through the branch to produce fruit is miraculous. When we translate the agrarian model into the spiritual realm, kingdom living goes to a whole new level.

The central truth of the branch abiding in the vine is the critical and deciding factor of whether fruit will be produced. The branch's continuous connection to the vine points to the mystical union of Christ and the believer. In the New Testament, this union is a dominant theme in the writings of the apostle Paul.

In Colossians 1:27–28, Paul describes this union as being "in Christ": "To them God has chosen to make known among the Gentiles the glorious riches of this mystery, which is Christ in you, the hope of glory. We proclaim him, admonishing and teaching everyone with all wisdom, so that we may present everyone perfect in Christ."

Galatians 2:20 is another example of how we are in union with Christ: "I have been crucified with Christ and I no longer live, but Christ lives in me. The life I live in the body, I live by faith in the Son of God, who loved me and gave himself for me."

When Jesus gave his parable about the vine and branch, his audience would have been familiar with the Old Testament Scripture in Isaiah 5, where it states that God planted choice vines (Israel) and managed the vineyard, only to find wild grapes at the time of harvest. Isaiah's parable talks about Israel's resistance against God's intention. In Jesus's parable, he is the true vine. This ensures that the driving force for grape produc-

tion is of the highest quality possible. As followers of Jesus, we are branches in union with the vine. God works as the gardener, and therefore everything necessary for fruit production is in place.

SOMETHING BETTER

Just as a grapevine does not produce fruit until its second year and matures over time in its ability to produce even better fruit, kingdom followers can look forward to a development process that allows them to honor God through increasingly better fruit production. The powerful influence of God's presence within us and our spiritual connection with him allows this process to work. Kingdom living is the experience of God as he not only resides in us but also flows through us.

Jesus personifies the vine by calling for the branches to "abide." In Spirit life, we must choose to abide (stay connected to Jesus) in the same way we choose to enter the small gate of the kingdom and make a choice to deal with competing weeds. Our choice to abide calls for continuous action.

THINGS WE CAN AND CAN'T DO

When Jesus says the branch can do nothing without him, he refers to our ability to produce fruit. However, the branch can stop fruit production by doing nothing.

As branches, we must remain sensitive to God's presence so he can be expressed spiritually through our lives. The goal is to allow God's Spirit to flow through us like sap moves from the vine through the branch.

The apostle Paul, in Romans 6, identifies this working of God's Spirit through our lives as a call to yield to the Spirit rather than to our sinful nature. "Do not yield your members to sin as instruments of wickedness, but yield yourselves to God as men who have been brought from death to life, and your members to God as instruments of righteousness" (RSV). However, this is not so easy.

Paul describes in Galatians 5:16–17 how God's Spirit and our sinful nature oppose each other in a way that creates a conflict. "So I say, live

by the Spirit, and you will not gratify the desires of the sinful nature. For the sinful nature desires what is contrary to the Spirit and the Spirit what is contrary to the sinful nature. They are in conflict with each other, so that you do not do what you want."

Our selfish nature resists the selfless, giving ways of God. As humans, we have an innate desire to protect and care for ourselves. It's a powerful driving force which isn't easily controlled. Giving up our selfish ways and choosing instead to follow God's self-giving nature produces a battle within us.

As kingdom followers, we must learn to shut the door to negative reflex reactions and quickly open the door to the movement of God. When we see the peace that is produced in our lives by saying no to our selfish, knee-jerk reactions to unpleasant people and situations, we are encouraged to more and more respond to the flow of God's Spirit.

A MIRACLE

Our ability to produce spiritual fruit depends on the miracle of God. It's like the process of fruit production which we observe in our natural world. Many unique things come together to allow this marvelous process. The first miracle is in the seed. God has prepackaged in the seed all the instructions needed for the miracle of growth to take place. The next miracle is the combination of sunlight, water, and soil that transfers nutrients to the plant. Just as fruit production cannot be accomplished in the darkness of a cave, the same holds true for spiritual fruit production as well.

"When Jesus spoke again to the people, he said, 'I am the light of the world. Whoever follows me will never walk in darkness, but will have the light of life'" (John 8:12). If you're not living in the light of Jesus, it's like expecting a plant to produce fruit in the darkness of a cave. If you think one hour of sunlight a week is enough light to keep the miracle going, try putting a plant in those conditions. The failure of your plant to survive will speak loudly about your Spirit life as well!

Without light, the fruit-bearing process is cut off. Our willingness to be exposed to God's light makes fruit possible. We can gain exposure

to God's light in many ways. Conversations with believers, personal Bible study, meditation, prayer, and corporate worship experiences are just a few of the sources of light available to us.

A PROCESS

Grape production is a process. In the early spring, the vine produces leaves to absorb the sunlight. Buds develop, followed by blooms that give the first evidence that fruit will follow.

Those sensitive to God learn quickly to notice blooms. They're the early signal that fruit is on the way. We need to identify the blooms of our sinful nature and pinch them off before the fruit of our behavior follows. Blooms of the Spirit that emerge at the gentle nudging of God must be protected and nourished.

Just as you need to control your selfish nature that pushes you to act or react, you must not let God's prompting be ignored. Many times you might sense God's desire for you to give of yourself to others, and yet the prompting never comes to fruit because the stress and strain of life distracts you. What began as a tug on your heart is soon forgotten.

God desires to express his love through you in countless ways. Speaking to someone who appears lonely, offering a helping hand, or giving of your resources to help those who barely survive under the demands of life are but a few. Even the simple things like a smile, a word of encouragement, or an e-mail can be avenues for God's love to reach others through you. Unless these blooms are nourished and protected, fruit never follows. You must make every effort not to allow good intentions to die on the vine.

QUICKER THAN WE CAN THINK

When it comes to our selfish natures, the movement from bloom to fruit is measured in seconds, not months. Self-fulfilling and self-protecting thoughts bloom, and negative actions follow quickly for those unskilled in Spirit life. However, for those who choose to live in God's presence, life is not a series of knee-jerk reactions. Awareness of God puts a different perspective on our otherwise selfish concerns.

One aspect of the fruit of the Spirit in our lives is self-control. James speaks to this when he says, "My dear brothers, take note of this: Everyone should be quick to listen, slow to speak and slow to become angry, for man's anger does not bring about the righteous life that God desires" (James 1:19). The ability to close the door to our self-nature and instead open the door to God (fast!) honors him and allows us to experience the quality of life he intends for us.

The goal is to allow spiritual fruit to work in our lives as fast as our knee-jerk reactions. When we learn to pull our responses from the Spirit rather than from our selfish nature, our knee-jerk responses take on a totally different character.

IMPORTANCE OF CONSCIENCE

Our conscience is a powerful tool to help us shut the door to self and open the door to God. Conscience is an inward urging that seeks to guide our actions and help us discern the quality of our thoughts. Conscience, coupled with the peace that comes from God's presence, is a mighty force to let us know when we are moving away from God.

Several places in the New Testament refer to the role of conscience in our relationship with the Father. Romans 2 describes people who keep the laws of God without actually knowing them. They fulfill the law as a response to their hearts and consciences. However, our conscience is not equal to God's Spirit.

In 1 Corinthians 6, Paul challenges Christians concerning their relationship with prostitutes. The conscience of these believers was not affected concerning this matter. In their culture, relationships with prostitutes were accepted. These believers needed their consciences expanded. Just because a person lacks the pain of conscience doesn't mean everything in his or her life is acceptable to God. In 1 Corinthians 4:4, Paul says, "My conscience is clear, but that does not make me innocent. It is the Lord who judges me."

The writer of Hebrews tells us that we should constantly be developing our ability to discern the appropriateness of what our lives are expressing. "But solid food is for the mature, who by constant use have

trained themselves to distinguish good from evil" (Hebrews 5:14). A conscience shaped by the Word can lead us in the ways of God as we are trained to distinguish good from evil. Our culture has the negative effect of making us comfortable with activities that are far from good. God's life-producing standards of good and evil are on a scale much higher than the self-gratification mantra promoted by our culture.

When it comes to discerning the source of what is stirring inside of you, James asks, "My brothers, can a fig tree bear olives, or a grapevine bear figs?" (James 3:12). His point is that a fig tree or grapevine produces fruit consistent with its nature. If what's moving in you doesn't conform to Jesus, slam the door!

Your desire to allow the expression of Jesus through your life will be fulfilled as you make fruit bearing your way of life. The call to abide in Jesus requires a continual connection. There are no special circumstances in which you should ask Jesus to sit still while you take care of some situation. Jesus is to always be the source of our actions and responses.

GOD'S NATURE REVEALED

If God were like us, he'd demand we get our act together! In all fairness, he'd bring into judgment everyone who fails to meet the standard of his requirements. However, God is not like humanity. Out of his nature of love, he gives the spiritual empowerment we need to experience life with him to its fullest.

Developing the level of kingdom life where God flows through us requires a deliberate choice to yield to God's desires rather than our own. Without anyone to give us guidance, it will require a lot of trial and error, as well as the resulting frustration. Take advantage of being a part of God's family. The help, companionship, and advice of other believers are invaluable as you seek to grow in your ability to let God flow through you. Those who have been down the road of life, paid attention, and purposefully sought to honor God have had experiences that will prove helpful to you. They can give you guidance as to how to stay in touch with God's peace and renew your mind so you don't simply react to situations, but rather allow God's love to flow through you.

Finding spiritual mentors isn't always easy. Look for people whose lives reflect peace, happiness, contentment, and the image of Christ. It will not be hard to notice those who are in touch with the heart of God.

SUPERNATURAL MOMENT

God's flowing through his followers is part of a string of miracles that make life in his kingdom possible. Our life with God reaches a supernatural level when we're born again, God makes his home with us, and God's presence flows through us. Jesus not only used the vine parable to emphasize this flow of God through us but also said, "Whoever believes in me, as the Scripture has said, streams of living water will flow from within him" (John 7:38). Sensitivity to the movement of God's Spirit in our lives is a life-changing miracle.

You can count on the fact that the desires, drives, and attitudes shaped by your life experiences will try to dominate your responses in difficult situations. You can start cooperating with God by consciously choosing to be slow to speak, checking for the correctness of your attitude and feelings, and refusing to be a tool of the devil by hurting others. By remaining sensitive to God's presence, you'll find it much easier to respectfully yield the right-of-way to him.

If we love God and desire to please him, our self-driven responses and actions will quickly become evident, but at the same time, God will enable us to overcome them. In his life, Jesus gave a vivid example of living in peace. No one was able to trick or entice him into doing wrong. He always responded deliberately and in a God-honoring way.

Any situation in which you'd normally respond in anger or frustration can be yielded to God, allowing him to flow in kindness, gentleness, and self-control in a supernatural moment. In a way, you become an observer of God's expressing himself through you. Such experiences are part of the life-giving and life-changing miracle of relationship with God.

THE WORK OF THE VITICULTURIST

Of course, the gardener is a major influence in this process. Breaking off dead branches, cutting back excess shoots, breaking up the ground to

add nutrients, applying water, and sometimes withholding water for the health of the vine are all parts his responsibility.

Spiritually, God as the vinedresser works with us in many ways. Dead branches are those things in our lives that feed our selfishness rather than serving God's purposes. When we draw close to Jesus and allow his teachings to confront us, our selfish ways appear in bold relief. By being honest with ourselves and trusting Jesus's life-giving ways, we allow God to remove the death-producing pieces of our lives.

The vinedresser cuts back stems and leaves to enhance fruit production, and this too has its parallel spiritually. When allowed to do so, God seeks to slow us down by removing some of the excess activities we are involved in which are not conducive to fruit bearing. We're all guilty of pouring a lot of energy and time into things that are simply not important or worthwhile. When God starts to cut them back, at first, we might feel we can't live without them. However, later we realize we weren't truly living because of them! When God is allowed to prioritize our lives, he will not leave us in the stress and strain that our choices create. We need to trust the vinedresser when he nudges us about the choices that occupy our time.

In the same way that the viticulturist feeds nutrients to the vine, God wants to feed us. Allowing God to open the ground of our lives so we can be fed requires a willingness to let him go deep within us as opposed to a simple surface touch. One important way God feeds us is through consistent study of his Word, which he can use to penetrate to the core of our identity. Over time, God's desire and purpose for us will replace the assessments of others, which can inflate our pride or damage our self-image. When we allow God to feed us at the core of our beings, he begins the miracle of accomplishing his purposes through us.

The viticulturist understands the balance of water needed for the health of the vine. In a similar way, God takes us through different seasons that seem at times to be harsh or inappropriate. He must be trusted through the dry and the rainy seasons of our lives.

By allowing God to identify and remove diseases and pests that destroy us, we cooperate with him as he fulfills his continuing work as the gardener. In the natural world, the destructive force of disease comes

at the vine in microscopic forms. In the spiritual realm, we're often severely challenged by dangerous forces that we never see coming. Ephesians 2 describes sources of death that we must seek God's help to defeat: the ways of the world, the tricks of the devil, our own desires, and destructive thinking.

Evaluating our way of life in a culture that runs counter to God demands some critical and reflective thinking. The subtle workings of the devil require us to have "night goggles" that allow us, with God's help, to see what's going on in the darkness. Dealing with our own destructive cravings demands that we depend upon the Holy Spirit's help to expose sources of death with the light of God.

Think about inviting a master viticulturist to take a look at the grapevine in your backyard. As he approaches your vine, he sees a world of things. He won't be able to wave his arms and offer a few instructions so that by the end of summer you have an award-winning crop of grapes. Rather, he'll see your grapevine as needing an unending process of change and attention, and it will take time to produce the full effect desired. Your trust is required to allow the master viticulturist to do his work by cutting green shoots, removing dead branches, and reshaping the entire vine. His work will allow the emergence of the fruit that is the miracle God intended—just like the miracle he planned when he first planted the seed of your life.

REFLECTING ON CHAPTER 9

Kingdom living is God in us and flowing through us. In what ways are you shutting the door to things that prevent God's miracle from happening? How can you open the door to things that allow the miracle to work?

Fruit production depends on exposure to light. What are the many sources of God's light that are available to you?

What specific situations come up in your life where you need to practice stopping the flow of self and yielding the right-of-way to God? What strategies do you have to accomplish this?

Chapter Ten

Experiencing the Trail

"EAT YOUR PEAS. FINISH YOUR SUPPER. No, you can't have ice cream. Brush your teeth. Get ready for bed. Stand up straight. Say thank you. Finish your homework. Clean your room. Wear your jacket. Take a bath. Be good to your brother. Show some respect. For goodness' sake, pay attention when I'm talking to you."

These instructions are all too familiar to anyone involved in the development of a child. The journey from childhood to adulthood is difficult. To encourage growth toward maturity, parents lovingly pour their best into their children in the areas of education, healthy habits, proper conduct, and so much more. Every possible source of positive input is utilized to promote the desired outcome. Parents who take their responsibility seriously agonize over whether their efforts will be in vain.

HORSES, WATER, AND SPIRITUAL MATURITY

In the country, folks often tell kids to "act like you have some raising." The expectation is that children should behave by the standard of what they've been taught, but often they don't. The familiar saying "you can lead a horse to water, but you can't make him drink" certainly applies here. Parents can't enforce or command maturity. It simply doesn't work.

In a similar way, our heavenly Father has the goal of spiritual maturity for us as his children. Everything we need for spiritual development is in place. However, God must wait until his desire for us becomes ours. The apostle Paul reinforces the importance of this personal decision

when he says, "When I became a man, I put childish ways behind me" (1 Corinthians 13:11b). Sadly, many people wait longer than they should to acknowledge the immaturity of their way of life.

FILLED WITH THE FULLNESS

The apostle Paul helps us see the essence of what maturing spiritually can achieve: "And I pray that you, being rooted and established in love, may have power, together with all the saints, to grasp how wide and long and high and deep is the love of Christ, and to know this love that surpasses knowledge—that you may be filled to the measure of all the fullness of God" (Ephesians 3:17b–19).

Those who have no desire for what God offers can be compared to someone who takes a trip to see the Great Smoky Mountains National Park and sits in the car rather than walking the trails. The opportunity to be filled with the fullness of God should draw us to explore and experience all that such an offer entails.

A MOUNTAIN TRAIL

Exploring a trail in the Smokies gives you the opportunity to see wildflowers, rhododendrons, mountain laurel, wildlife, pristine streams, waterfalls, native trout, towering trees, and vistas that will take your breath away. Surely you're not going to stay in the car and sleep! There is so much to see and do! Yet, even with so much available, many never experience all that the mountains offer.

I was blessed to grow up within a thirty-minute drive of the Great Smoky Mountains National Park. There's a great deal I could tell you about things to see and experience there. But more importantly, I've explored the trails of the kingdom, and these trails offer you life-changing and life-giving experiences with God. These trails ensure a life of more than just chasing moments—a life that is full and replete with the presence of God.

Throughout this book, I've mentioned a continuous array of spiritual opportunities. The peace of God's presence, the power of his Spirit to shape us, the renewal of our minds, and the shepherding guidance of

the Spirit are but a few of the ways God desires to help us develop toward spiritual maturity. But at some point, you must spiritually get out of the car. You must have the faith to take God up on his offer of a personal, spiritual relationship. When you desire what he desires for you, your life is supernaturally transformed.

Through a relationship with God, we gain the spiritual empowerment to defeat the things that take life from us and embrace the things that give us life. Every mountain trail that appears daunting at first is accomplished one step at a time. The same holds true for growing into the fullness of spiritual maturity. The first step is your decision to pursue rather than refuse God's desire to take you to a new level of life spiritually.

A Craving for More

Peter describes a key element of this process: "Like newborn babies, crave pure spiritual milk, so that by it you may grow up in your salvation, now that you have tasted that the Lord is good" (1 Peter 2:2–3).

Peter says that even the smallest encounter with God should produce a hunger for more. For most people, it only takes a taste of something sweet to stir a craving for all we can have. Surely, the same should hold true with God.

Peter's words reinforce the point that nothing is ever as convincing as personal experience. No matter how eloquently we describe the benefits of a new food to our children, many of them hate it without trying it. We face a difficult battle until we're able to maneuver a taste into the child's mouth. Once a taste reveals how good the food is, they usually crave for more.

I like Peter's use of the word "crave." Think of pizza, chocolate, or ice cream. The idea of having such an intense desire for God is a stretch for those who only go to church to make sure the deal with God about life after death stays paid up.

Feeding the Pets

The concept of craving for God is illustrated vividly for me when I feed our pets. Cats are frustrating, because they might take a hesitant bite or

even ignore what I place in front of them as if offended that there's not something better. On the other hand, feeding my Labrador retriever is a treat. Lady meets me as I'm carrying her food, bouncing all over the place with eager anticipation for whatever's in her bowl. She eats as if I'm going to take it back before she's finished or like it's the last meal she'll ever get. It is a genuine pleasure to feed her.

How does God view our spiritual craving for him? Do we take a taste with the tip of our tongue, or do we show up with a huge bowl? Do we seek only a taste of spiritual milk, or do we want a constant flow so that the full potential of spiritual growth can be accomplished?

The treetop experience described in chapter 1 was a taste—a small experience—of God. When we pursue rather than ignore such moments, we discover God's great plan for us. Climbing trees isn't for everyone, so your experience with God will be unique to who you are. The important thing is to recognize the vastness of God's touch on your life. These moments may be simple and brief, but if you respond rather than reject them, you're giving God the opportunity to achieve his desire of filling you with his fullness.

Deeper Into the Mountains

Some, in fear of getting lost, never consider a mountain trail. In the same way, many are uneasy about God's spiritual realm. They wrongly consider encounters with God to be for other people—those with a pioneer spirit. However, each time we venture into God's spiritual realm, we gain the confidence to go even further the next time. Each small experience with God gives a longing for more. It's how we mature spiritually—one step at a time.

It's up to you to decide how far you want to go spiritually. The previous chapter offered the challenge of producing spiritual fruit by allowing God to flow through you. The ability to live in this dimension of Spirit life requires time and maturity. Each occasion of yielding in obedience to God's ways or allowing him to love on others through you builds you progressively toward spiritual maturity.

Just as some people don't want anything more of the mountains

than a ride through the park, unfortunately there are some whose only contact with the kingdom is through an occasional trip to church. Just as riding through the park is certainly worth the trip, church is also worth the time and effort. However, the magnificence of the kingdom is to be experienced personally and then brought back to be enjoyed corporately.

TRAIL REPORTS

According to the book of Acts, God was glorified in the events of Paul's missionary journeys, and when he returned, he celebrated with the local churches. Our church life should be filled with these same kinds of reports to inspire and encourage others in their journey.

Experiencing the kingdom only from the vantage point of church is like waiting in the car to hear from others about their time on a trail. In church, it's a joy to hear reports of how God has changed people's lives or guided them in the ways they should go. Even further, it is encouraging to hear of the numerous occasions in the Scriptures when God did wonderful things with his people. Yet, the good news is that we're not left in the car waiting to hear from others. We have the opportunity to personally travel the trails of the kingdom.

PARTICIPANTS, NOT SPECTATORS

To get out on the trail, we have an obstacle to overcome. We are part of a spectator, "entertain me" consumer culture. God's invitation is to be participants, not spectators; to be givers rather than consumers. "What's in it for me?" is to be replaced by "How can I help someone else?" Kingdom followers seek to produce life-giving experiences for others. It's the way of God. It's what allows us to grow up spiritually.

Life with God means that we get to experience a mountain-stream crossing for ourselves. We get to feel the cold water that takes our breath away, hear the sound of the water, smell the freshness, and experience the stream's power. When you allow God to flow through you, it will take your breath away. By living in God's kingdom, you'll be sensitive to a whole new world of freshness around you. The press of God upon your

heart will be like the power of a mountain stream that wants to carry you along with it.

The path to spiritual maturity will put you in touch with many new experiences. Paul writes about the peace of God that goes beyond his ability to understand (Philippians 4:7). He speaks of contentment in all circumstances, whether easy or hard (Philippians 4:11). His assessment that nothing surpasses the greatness of knowing Jesus as Lord is a reality available to be experienced by everyone, as opposed to merely being words on a page (Philippians 3:8).

When you travel a mountain trail, away from the city, pollution, and the modern world, you get to see how God made our world in the beginning. The grandeur and life-sustaining order of nature is obvious and powerful. Similarly, by opening yourself up to being changed through the power of God's indwelling Spirit, you catch a glimpse of what humanity was like before selfishness, greed, and pleasure seeking took over.

Our willingness to be obedient to God's ways and consequently experience more of his life will create a desire in us to keep getting out of the car to travel more of the trails of the kingdom. For example, choosing to be slow to speak rather than quick to respond offers you the opportunity to understand the needs and hurts of others that cause them to lash out, rather than the excuse for you to dish out what they deserve. Walking with God gives you a mountaintop perspective of how life is to be lived.

CHALLENGES OF THE TRAIL

When you are hiking a mountain trail, there are hills to negotiate which require pushing hard to make it up the next rise. At times, a swarm of bees can ruin your day. An occasional bear is exciting to see, but it can be life-threatening to get between her and her cubs.

We also face hills and valleys spiritually. Sometimes they are occasions when God's timing doesn't match ours. We might find that being patient in the face of someone's anger doesn't always turn a situation around as quickly as we'd like. The trail seems to turn straight up a hill when we're tempted to retaliate rather than trust God's ways. This can

happen often in a marriage relationship. Sometimes one spouse lags behind in spiritual development, making it hard for the other spouse not to become impatient.

Bees and bears can distract us from our walk with God. However, as Paul says in Romans 5:3–5, "Not only so, but we also rejoice in our sufferings, because we know that suffering produces perseverance; perseverance, character; and character, hope. And hope does not disappoint us, because God has poured out his love into our hearts by the Holy Spirit, whom he has given us." Sometimes people are mean. Situations can be unfair. We must be careful not to let difficult circumstances cause us to give up on the whole idea of mountain hiking—after all, some Christians even die for the faith. God is available to us in hard times, so we need to look beyond the moment.

Every backcountry trail, waterfall, mountain stream, and canopy of fall colors creates a yearning in me to never lose touch with God. Perhaps you can relate to that feeling. Equally so, your experience of each life-changing and life-giving way of the kingdom can create a longing in you to keep opening your Bible and your heart so that God can take you further up the mountain.

A Yearning Heart

God's yearning heart for his children is expressed by Jeremiah: "For I know the plans I have for you,' declares the Lord, 'Plans to prosper you and not to harm you, plans to give you hope and a future. Then you will call upon me and come and pray to me, and I will listen to you. You will seek me and find me when you seek me with all your heart'" (Jeremiah 29:11–13).

Just as parents have hopes and dreams for their children, God has hopes and dreams for us. In both cases, we must make a personal decision to embrace the goal. By seeing the value of maturity, our children incorporate what we as parents spend a lifetime trying to show them. In the same way, when we see the value of God's kingdom and yield to his shepherding, we allow him to complete his desire to fill us with his fullness.

MAKING THE CHOICE

Most parents would faint if their child took his favorite toy to a friend saying, "Here, you play with it for a while, because it would give me greater pleasure to watch you having fun than playing with it myself." Parents would be shocked if their child said, "No, I don't want ice cream because it would ruin my supper."

Maturity is a choice, a personal decision not to be ruled by childish attitudes. For Christians, this means living like Jesus. It's being deliberate rather than impulsive, and God-centered rather than me-centered. It's a self-imposed standard of identifying ourselves in Christ. The result of spiritual maturity is that we keep our focus on God rather than running from one desire to the next.

The willingness and desire to keep responding to God's touch opens the door for a fuller encounter with him. Moses could have dismissed his burning-bush experience and walked away: instead, he spent a lifetime pressing in to God's presence and ways. Have you possibly failed to recognize thoughts or experiences that were larger than life? Are you sensitive to God's call for you to come higher up the mountain with him?

Language has limitations. It's difficult to describe adequately all that is involved in being filled with the fullness of God. Our decision to pursue all God offers opens the door to possibilities that nothing in life can match.

MORE TRAILS TO TRAVEL

Maturity is a lifelong pursuit. We never fully arrive, but are always reaching for the goal. The saying "It takes a village to raise a child" is true in the kingdom as well. The varied spiritual gifting of God's people helps us grow together "until we all reach unity in the faith and in the knowledge of the Son of God and become mature, attaining to the whole measure of the fullness of Christ" (Ephesians 4:13).

One measure of maturity is the humility to be taught by others and hold respect for those whose lives evidence that they know God. Surrounding yourself with those who love to walk the trails of God's king-

dom brings mutual enjoyment and encouragement in the pursuit of the fullness of God.

The question remains whether you desire what he desires for you. I join with Paul in praying that you will come to understand and experience the immeasurable depth of God's love for you and his desire to fill you.

Reflecting on Chapter 10

Maturity is a choice, a personal decision not to be ruled by childish attitudes. In what areas of your life do you struggle to grow up into the ways of God?

Getting out of the car and exploring kingdom trails with God is the difference in being a spectator and a participant. In what areas of your Christian life are you a spectator? A participant?

In what ways have you witnessed those living in the kingdom demonstrating a craving for God?

Are you involved in the mutual experience of sharing your kingdom experiences with other believers on a regular basis? How has this helped you to mature in your faith?

Chapter Eleven

A Day in the Kingdom

EARLIER I MENTIONED MY GRANDSON Nathanael's training regimen for becoming the man in the field. The desire of his heart inspired him to train so that he could realize his dream. Just wanting to be the man in the field wasn't enough. Taking action was required. With something vastly more important in front of us—fullness of life in God's kingdom—it's our turn to make a move.

Our entrance into the kingdom begins by being born again. As was described in earlier chapters, this spiritual birth is the beginning step toward additional spiritual possibilities. Unless we mature beyond this initial event, the ability to remain aware of God or let him flow through us will not be achieved. Equally so, the benefits of God being our shepherd are not realized unless we invest ourselves in getting to know his voice in the various ways he guides and touches our lives.

How does one live in God's kingdom? What is kingdom life like on a daily basis? What things need to be done to maximize our acceptance of what God offers?

A variety of activities occupy the lives of kingdom citizens. From a relational standpoint, we seek to make the kingdom visible to others by honoring Jesus in our words and actions. We constantly try to be sensitive to God's gentle prompting as he seeks to express himself through us. Rather than living by the assumed standards of our culture, we look critically at the many automatic actions or activities to which we're accustomed. Instead of our lives being a reflection of the current fads and

trends of our world, we seek to live in the uniqueness of the way Jesus lived.

At first glance, this could come across as quite a day's work! Tending to all of these spiritual issues while trying to make a living, complete an education, take care of a family, or just survive life might seem overwhelming. The need to shut the door to sinful behaviors, open the door to God's flow, and constantly challenge our cultural way of life appears to require constant attention. When is there time to just relax and enjoy life?

TRAIN TO BE GODLY

Paul told Timothy, "Train yourself to be godly" (1 Timothy 4:7b). Training (practicing discipline) is a principle of kingdom life. The benefits of training to be godly can be compared to the benefits of practicing your golf swing, conditioning yourself before running a race, or mastering the skills of piloting a plane.

Until training establishes a natural response and confidence in us, each of these enterprises will be hard work and not much fun! However, through practice, the multiple components of a golf swing can be mastered in such a way that you're enjoying the game as opposed to constantly rehearsing everything required to execute a proper swing. When you experience a runner's high or finish a marathon with energy to spare, running becomes a passion instead of strenuous exercise. The joy of flying a plane on a beautiful summer day with visibility for miles is yours because of the confidence training gives. That's after a steady calmness replaces your death grip on the controls and the uncertainty of whether you'll make it home alive!

RELAX AND ENJOY THE RIDE

When we train to be godly, a day in the kingdom becomes a constant joy. If we train properly, the power of God's Spirit transforms our old habits so we can relax and enjoy the ride.

In some ways, training to be godly is like learning to hit a golf ball. The golf swing is not a natural movement. You can prove this by giving

an average person a golf club and asking him or her to hit the ball! In a similar way, the dynamics of Spirit life are not easily mastered. However, with training, the golf club becomes a natural extension of the body. The same outcome is possible for your Spirit life. Just remember, the ability to honor Christ with your life demands the discipline and effort of training.

All wannabe golfers, runners, and pilots want the end results I've described. Yet, many are unwilling to put forth the effort to train so they can realize their goal. By comparison, most Christians want their lives to honor God. However, without training to be godly, life for them is constant trial-and-error frustration.

What follows is not an exhaustive treatment of how to train to be godly, but rather a start. Perfecting any endeavor requires a consistent and long-term effort. The same holds true for kingdom living.

MASTER THE FUNDAMENTALS

Everyone who's tried to play golf has first had to understand the fundamentals of a good swing. Equally so, understanding the fundamentals is important for Spirit life.

I learned the components of a good golf swing by being a caddy, the one who carries the bag for the player. Years of caddying for people who didn't play well ingrained in me what didn't work. However, occasionally I'd have the opportunity to caddy for someone who was a credit to the game. There was a stark difference in what I saw. Observing good players imprinted the proper swing in my mind. After the correct image was set firmly in my head, I had opportunity to convert that image into action through practice.

Years later, I became the assistant to a golf pro and gave lessons to those who were just beginning to play. Helping others master the fundamentals of the game gave me a lot of satisfaction.

Before swinging a golf club, your body must be in the correct position with the clubface square on the ball in correct alignment to the desired line of flight. Just as setup is crucial in golf, it's also crucial when it comes to kingdom life. God is the shepherd, and you are the one who

listens for his voice. God must be set squarely in front of every event of life.

Additional pieces of a good golf swing involve keeping your head down, staying relaxed, and executing smooth motions. The swing begins by making the proper turn of your body as you cock your wrists. While staying in balance, the downswing begins with the turn of the hips and the releasing of the wrists as you put the clubhead on the ball, continuing with a proper follow-through.

Life in the Spirit has a similar dynamic. Keep your head down in humility and reverence for God as your shepherd. Relax and let God's ways flow rather than using reflex reactions. Stay in balance, and make the proper turn by shutting the door to selfish impulses and opening the door to God. Like putting the clubhead on the ball, apply God's Word to every event in life, using the proper follow-through all the way without taking situations back under selfish control.

RENEWING YOUR MIND

The ability to visualize is important for golfing, running, piloting a plane, and many other activities requiring mind-body coordination. The power of the mind to work with the body to execute what we picture can't be emphasized strongly enough. That's why it's important to study, train, and perfect the movements we seek to acquire. The same is true for kingdom living.

Paul writes, "Do not conform any longer to the pattern of this world, but be transformed by the renewing of your mind. Then you will be able to test and approve what God's will is—his good, pleasing and perfect will" (Romans 12:2a). To renew our minds is to train in godliness. This begins with our thought lives.

The damaging reflex reactions that so quickly become our first response to situations are the product of how we've trained our minds. We often say we did something without thinking. However, that's not completely true. A rapid mental process occurred to assess the situation and formulate a response. This process was based on previous experiences or accepted ways of thinking that we have accumulated in life.

As a parent, I remember responding to my son in a discipline situation in the same way that my dad did with me. As a child, I hated my dad's response. Yet, I repeated it with my son. Why? My mind assessed the situation in a split second, and my response was dictated by my past experiences.

Such incidents are reminders of the importance of never acting rashly. But even more, they demonstrate our need to renew our minds. Our mental picture of how we should act as godly parents needs to be so strong that our minds don't race ahead of what is spiritually correct.

When I worked at a home for juvenile boys, their image of what constitutes manhood had been formed out of their life experiences. The image was not only wrong, but was also the source of much pain in their lives. We worked to help them renew their minds. Our goal was to give them a different mental image that could become the source of appropriate actions. If they heard a concept once, it did not accomplish our goal. Continual practice and the desire to change were required so they could make progress in replacing old ways with life-giving images and actions.

As Christians, we need to renew our minds with the many examples of godly living that are available to us in the Scriptures. Our minds need to be saturated with the model of how Jesus lived, accompanied by the passion to be like him. Even professional golfers must renew their minds to be successful. They can't execute what they can't visualize. They'll also easily revert to old habits unless they're driven by the conviction that only the proper swing really works consistently.

The transformation of the mind involves a process. Paul gives us encouragement not to lose heart in this effort: "And we, who with unveiled faces all reflect the Lord's glory, are being transformed into his likeness with ever-increasing glory, which comes from the Lord, who is the Spirit" (2 Corinthians 3:18).

Renewal Through Study

One way to renew your mind is to study the life of Jesus. For example, read through the gospel of John, and pay close attention to how Jesus

responds to people. Having read these accounts when you were ten years old is not enough to imprint them upon your mind or remind you to apply them in present-day situations.

Most Christians are hard-pressed to give much detail as to how Jesus lived. Success in honoring God with our lives depends upon reading the Word carefully and consistently, and visualizing and admiring the Master in action. Serious golfers benefit from master players who give them a mental picture of the correct swing. We benefit from knowing how our Shepherd lived out life in the kingdom.

KEEPING SCORE ON OURSELVES

After a challenging situation occurs, ask yourself, "Was the way I handled this indicative of how Jesus dealt with life?" The answer first of all requires the knowledge of how Jesus dealt with life. Secondly, the ability to follow his example depends on a passion to be like him. This results from the confidence that his "swing" is the one that gives life—as opposed to our natural responses, which bring conflict, problems, destruction, and death.

During the training phase, golfing students often start the swing properly but revert to old habits at some point during the swing. For those involved in kingdom training, the same thing happens. You might start hand in hand with God in dealing with a situation and then revert to what you think will work better. For example, no matter how many times anger doesn't work, some people keep going back to this damaging response as if they never learned how to do life properly. Practice is crucial, so don't give up.

SEEING MORE CLEARLY

Playing a round of golf with a pro, taking a run with an Olympic athlete, or flying second-seat with a seasoned pilot are thrills for students with a passion for learning. It's not easy to notice every motion and action a pro executes. The untrained eye never sees all the details that hours of practice and study bring into view. With just a touch that is not obvious to the student, the seasoned pilot is able to keep the flight smooth. You

might already be aware of the fundamentals involved in your running or golf game, but a pro can surprise you by quickly identifying small adjustments you need to make.

Professional golfers didn't start out with the perfect swing. Like many of us, they too have had to break old habits and renew their minds. Through practice, the diligent student doesn't have to be reminded not to jump off the ground when swinging, because the right mental picture would never allow such a thing. Training in godliness gives us the same promise of change. As our minds are renewed, Jesus becomes the dominating mental picture. Jesus can even become our automatic reaction. Through proper training in godliness, we won't jump off the ground in anger, envy, willfulness, or addictive behavior when dealing with a life situation of any kind. By renewing our minds, we ensure that Jesus will not be discredited by our old habits.

Let's use the teaching of James as an example of training in godliness: "My dear brothers, take note of this: Everyone should be quick to listen, slow to speak and slow to become angry, for man's anger does not bring about the righteous life that God desires" (James 1:19–20). When an intense situation arises, defense and retaliation pound on the door, wanting to be expressed. At first, it takes a conscious effort to hold ourselves back. The moment feels strange. We're not quite sure how all this works. It feels as unnatural as trying to keep a plane level in flight. We start off well by practicing patience, but usually it doesn't take long before we return to our damaging old habits. The same old thing results: hurt and pain to all involved. When will we ever learn that anger is not a solution?

The next time a challenging situation arises, we're in a position to benefit from our previous mistakes. Our ability to hang on in patience and understanding rather than retaliating has been strengthened by our desire not to repeat past failures. Sometimes we're fortunate, and the situation changes quickly before we lose our ability to hold on. "Wow, God's ways do work! His ways bring life so I don't mess up my relationships! I've got it!"

It would be nice if we were able to master our responses that quickly

and continue getting great results. However, the previous example is like the golfing student who hits a shot that would make any pro proud. The shot was amazing, but the student is far from being ready to sign up for the pro tour. All who play the game know that the next three shots after that kind of success may make the same person want to give up the game.

The same is true for training in godliness. Occasionally we might open the door to Jesus and experience the life he brings, but we're still far from having a mind that is fully renewed. Many more practice sessions and even a few one-on-one lessons from a pro will help tremendously. Spending time with and learning from Christians who are true representatives of the faith will help you reach the goal you envision much more quickly.

And of course, responding to God as he lives in your life will do that and much more. The joy of allowing God to transform death into life in you—and bless those around you as a result—will keep you training in godliness. Once you allow the image of God to dominate your mental picture of every situation, you are well on the way to accomplishing your goal of a God-honoring life.

Attention to Detail

As in playing golf, perfecting your running style, or piloting a plane, attention to detail is important. Sometimes the smallest detail can make a huge difference. By avoiding carelessness in your approach to spirituality, you honor God, and your training allows him to flow through you every time. Athletes do not train haphazardly or occasionally if they hope to perfect their sport. Surely, we want to give even greater attention to detail in our approach to spiritual maturity.

Visualizing the model of life in Christ is but one dimension of renewing our minds. Paul adds another dimension: "Finally, brothers, whatever is true, whatever is noble, whatever is right, whatever is pure, whatever is lovely, whatever is admirable—if anything is excellent or praiseworthy—think about such things. Whatever you have learned or received or heard from me, or seen in me—put it into practice. And the God of

peace will be with you" (Philippians 4:8–9). If our minds are saturated with things honorable before God, our actions will be drawn from a source that is pure and life-giving for everyone involved.

Earlier, I mentioned the misconception that kingdom living requires a constantly alert status, never relaxing or enjoying life in order to constantly make sure we open the door to God and close it to our selfish natures. The reality is that through training and confidence in the life-producing ways of God, life in the kingdom becomes a natural expression of our changed lives.

Paul says that someone far stronger than us stands guard: "And the peace of God, which transcends all understanding, will guard your hearts and your minds in Christ Jesus" (Philippians 4:7).

THE THRILL OF VICTORY

A number of years ago during the coverage of the Olympics, the phrase "the thrill of victory and the agony of defeat" was repeated often. Nothing matches an athlete's euphoria at seeing the triumphant results of the commitment to continue with lonely workouts, persevere through injuries, and push until the body almost breaks. In that moment, training comes to fulfillment in the sport that the athlete loves and has made the central focus of his or her life.

When honoring God becomes your central focus, there's no greater thrill than seeing your spiritual training expressed in a moment that transforms a situation from death to life. Spiritually, the agony of defeat is a great burden to carry when, in a time of great need, God is dishonored, people are hurt, and the devil is able to take the victor's stand. But take heart—it does not need to end in failure. The joy you can look forward to is that through the discipline of training and the guidance of the Holy Spirit, your mind can be renewed to choose God's ways as your first response. As a result of effort in training, God's ways become a natural, integral part of your life. For those who train, a day in the kingdom is not work. It's the pleasure of doing something that has become the passion of their lives.

Golfers, runners, and pilots will tell you that the joy of what they do

is a direct result of their training efforts. The same holds true for kingdom living. Paul's words to Timothy are appropriate for us to hear once again: "Train yourself to be godly. For physical training is of some value, but godliness has value for all things, holding promise for both the present life and the life to come" (1 Timothy 4:7b–8).

Reflecting on Chapter 11

What motivates you to train for spiritual maturity?

Based on the example of Jesus, how should we live our daily lives?

Have you ever been in a spiritual training regimen? By what means?

Having read this chapter, are there any additional things you will do in your pursuit of spiritual maturity?

In what ways can your church help you to train for spiritual maturity?

Chapter Twelve

Larger Than Life

THE WORLD OF ADVERTISING constantly bombards us with extraordinary claims. In an attempt to stir a got-to-have-it fever in the marketplace, phrases like "cutting-edge technology," "best price," and "superior quality" are used to promote products. It can be challenging to sort through the hype of these marketing ploys. After all, ad campaigns are often overstated.

A lot happened during the decades after the death and resurrection of Jesus. Paul completed his three missionary journeys and later was killed. Jerusalem was attacked, and the temple was destroyed by the Romans. The persecution of Christians eased occasionally and at other times intensified. False teachings invaded the church, and tough economic times made it difficult for the early Christians to survive.

The apostle John was present when Jesus spoke of the kingdom as being good news, the priceless pearl, and the path to life. For more than fifty years, John worked to continue what Jesus had started. Toward the end of his life, he was exiled as a prisoner to the island of Patmos. What impact did those fifty years have on John? Was he discouraged? Did he feel that Jesus had overstated his claims?

"OUT OF THIS COUNTRY"

At a point toward the end of his life, John wrote, "How great is the love the Father has lavished on us, that we should be called children of God! And that is what we are! ...Dear friends, now we are children of God,

and what we will be has not yet been made known. But we know that when he appears, we shall be like him, for we shall see him as he is" (1 John 3:1a, 2).

John's excitement becomes more evident when we explore the language in which he originally wrote. His phrase "how great," when literally translated, conveys the expression, "Behold in astonishment the out-of-this-country love the Father has lavished on us!" Speaking of the Father's love being "lavished" carries the idea of a gift given in great abundance. John's euphoria reaches even higher when he says that we should be "called the children of God! And that is what we are!" Though it seems nothing could top what he just said, he indicates that there's still more to come. Our future in Christ will be much greater than what we're enjoying now.

For John, "good news," "priceless pearl," and "path to life" are not overstated claims. In fact, Jesus's words are modest in comparison to what John experienced. Even in the face of persecution, hard times, and the battle with false teaching, John's words are his testimony that a relationship with God is an unfathomable opportunity.

What could possibly make John feel this way? How did he manage to keep the difficulties of life from robbing him of his joy in following Jesus? Did he have or know something we don't?

We know with certainty that John understood the principles of life in God's kingdom. In fact, John's gospel teaches us many things about the kingdom that the other gospel writers fail to mention. We've often referred to the gospel of John in this book to introduce many kingdom principles: choosing to be born again, allowing God to make his home in us, following the leading of the Good Shepherd, and giving opportunity for God to be expressed through us as a vine and branch. All of these concepts can be summed up in one final concept from John's gospel: *zoe*.

Zoe

John's relationship with God gave a special quality to life that nothing in the outside world could take away. John made certain that we would know the truth about the kingdom. He tells us in John 20:31, "But these are written that you may believe that Jesus is the Christ, the Son of God,

and that by believing you may have life in his name."

The New Testament makes a distinction between the life that Jesus came to give and simply being alive. Just as we have many ways in the English language to describe life, the Greek New Testament uses multiple words when referring to life.

The following example from John 10 demonstrates how the New Testament writers came to reserve the Greek word *zoe* (zo-ay) to refer to the special quality of life Jesus offers. "I have come that they may have life [zoe] and have it to the full" (John10:10b). Every human being possesses life, animation, and vitality. In Jesus there is fullness of life—the *zoe* experience of connection with God. More than mere existence, this special, vibrant quality that makes life wonderfully dynamic and meaningful comes from God. "For as the Father has life [zoe] in himself, so he has granted the Son to have life [zoe] in himself" (John 5:26).

IMMEASURABLY MORE

If the principles of the kingdom become your way of life, Paul's words in Ephesians 3:20–21 will be fulfilled in you: "Now to him who is able to do immeasurably more than all we ask or imagine, according to his power that is at work within us, to him be glory in the church and in Christ Jesus throughout all generations, for ever and ever! Amen."

We use the cliché "the sky's the limit" to describe things that have endless possibilities. Paul's statement about God's ability to do more than we can ask or imagine certainly sets the stage for an exciting future. When we allow God to work within us, he is glorified, and we experience a quality of life that only relationship with him can bring.

Many have gone before us, and others are yet to come to experience life in God's kingdom. Jesus said in Matthew 13:45–46, "Again, the kingdom of heaven is like a merchant looking for fine pearls. When he found one of great value, he went away and sold everything he had and bought it." How about you? Have you found that the kingdom is an out-of-this-world opportunity you don't want to miss?

An eternal future with God is available to all who see what many others pass by. Responding to the kingdom invitation is a life-changing

journey that's also life-giving. Only through the kingdom is there *zoe*—the special quality of life with our Creator and Lord.

A WARNING AND A PROMISE

I close with the warning given in the beginning of this book: saying "Lord, Lord" is not enough, because religious actors will be rejected. Most people are on the road to destruction, and few ever find the small gate and narrow road that lead to life. You must not only live in the kingdom, but the King must also live in you. Be relentless in your pursuit of God, and let nothing hinder you. The fullness of life awaits you.

Choosing the kingdom is a decision based on desire, not fear of punishment. Therefore, I also close with a promise: life in all its fullness awaits you! This is the larger-than-mere-existence miracle Jesus came to give. There are mountains to climb, rivers to cross, and adventures beyond description ready for you as you adhere closely to the narrow road of God's kingdom.

ENCOURAGEMENT FOR YOUR TRAVELS

Over the past two thousand years, a great number of people have left the broad path in order to travel the narrow road of the kingdom. Some have enjoyed the fullness of kingdom living, while others haven't. Therefore, remember that you must deal with weeds—competing desires to the kingdom way of life. The pH of your life must be kept in proper balance, because Jesus must increase while you decrease. There's also the need to constantly reseed your life with the word of the kingdom so that you can enjoy a full harvest. Only if you train to be godly will you learn to live by the empowerment of God's Spirit. Life in the kingdom requires discipline, desire, and the willingness to fight against powers within us and outside of us.

Paul's statement in Ephesians 3:20 that God "is able to do immeasurably more than we can ask or imagine, according to his power at work within us" points to the possibilities that await kingdom followers. Your consistency in living the way of the kingdom determines to what degree you will experience what is available.

Jesus ended his parable of the sower with these words: "Others, like

seed sown on good soil, hear the word, accept it, and produce a crop—thirty, sixty or even a hundred times what was sown" (Mark 4:20). By normal standards, a return of ten times on the seed planted would be a great harvest, but Jesus projects the mind-blowing possibilities available in the kingdom. If you hear and accept the word of the kingdom and deal with the competing weeds and distractions that come your way, fullness of life is yours at a level far beyond what you can imagine.

The blessing given in Hebrews 13:20–21 is my prayer for you: "May the God of peace, who through the blood of the eternal covenant brought back from the dead our Lord Jesus, that great Shepherd of the sheep, equip you with everything good for doing his will, and may he work in us what is pleasing to him, through Jesus Christ, to whom be glory for ever and ever. Amen."

I offer the following as a challenge to inspire you to go to the top of the mountain with God.

> If I am motivated,
> my discipline will be in order.
> If I am disciplined,
> my motivation will find opportunity.

REFLECTING ON CHAPTER 12

The apostle John was a living example of Jesus's claims concerning the worth of the kingdom. What is your personal testimony as to the worth of the kingdom?

How would you explain to someone else the *zoe* quality of life of the kingdom?

If *zoe* life in the kingdom and your relationship with the Lord are located at due north, where have you strayed from the trail, sat to rest with too much satisfaction, or seen an artificial summit?

Having read this book, what do you plan to do with what you have learned?